Adamczyk, Alice J.,
1942-

Black dance

$29.00

DATE			

BLACK DANCE

GARLAND REFERENCE LIBRARY
OF THE HUMANITIES
(VOL. 558)

Dance Theater of Harlem   *Martha Swope*
"Serenade"
Dancers: Lowell Smith, Stephanie Dabney, Virginia Johnson
             Schomburg Center for Research in Black Culture
                    The New York Public Library
                 Astor, Lenox and Tilden Foundations

BLACK DANCE
An Annotated Bibliography

Alice J. Adamczyk

GARLAND PUBLISHING, INC. • NEW YORK & LONDON
1989

Library of Congress Cataloging-in-Publication Data

Adamczyk, Alice J., 1942–
    Black dance : an annotated bibliography / Alice J. Adamcyzk.
        p. cm. — (Garland reference library of the humanities ; vol.
    558)
    Includes index.
    ISBN 0–8240–8808–5 (alk. paper)
    1. Blacks—Dancing—Bibliography. I. Title. II. Series.
Z7514.D2A33   1989
[GV1595]
016.7933'2—dc19   88-29217
                                                            CIP

Printed on acid-free, 250-year-life paper
Manufactured in the United States of America

CONTENTS

v

Gonzell White's Jazzers   *Earl Brody*

ACKNOWLEDGMENTS

Acknowledgments go to the following people who helped make this book possible: Richard Newman, now of the New York Public Library's Publications Office, who encouraged me by signing me with Garland Publishing and giving me citations and suggestions; Sharon M. Howard, Assistant Acquisitions Librarian at the Schomburg Center for Research in Black Culture, for making me aware of new publications on black dance; Betty Gubert, Head of General Research and Reference Collections, Schomburg Center, who contributed significantly by spending many hours helping to proofread and edit the manuscript; the staff of the General Research Division and the Dance Collection of the New York Public Library for their efficient service; the staff of the Schomburg Center for their assistance and encouragement, especially Assistant Chief Catherine J. Lenix-Hooker, Publications Officer Glenderlyn Johnson, Deborah Willis of Exhibitions, Mario Charles and Sharon Robinson of General Research and Reference Collections, Acquisitions Librarian Valerie Sandoval Mwalilino, Deirdre Bibby of the Art, Prints, and Artifacts Section, and Victor Smythe and Sule Greg Wilson of the Rare Books, Manuscripts and Archives Section. Special thanks go to George Hill, Albert Murray, and Joe Nash for giving me material and suggestions.

Juba at Vauxhall Gardens, London, from *Illustrated London News*
(August 5, 1848)

INTRODUCTION

Dance as a means of expression is one of the oldest art forms. It probably existed before music and may well be its source as well as the source of all other art forms. It exists in all cultures and is performed for social, ceremonial, theatrical, and religious reasons. The Africans who came to Latin America, the Caribbean and the United States as slaves brought with them their own social, ceremonial, and religious dances. Over the centuries these slaves' descendants developed rituals and ceremonies, both social and religious, using dance as a medium of expression. Though rooted in the New World their dance derived from Africa.

This bibliography is the first attempt to compile published material documenting black dance in all of its forms. The compilation shows the extent of black involvement in dance and also how that involvement has influenced and become a part of the various cultures and idioms of the New World. The field of black dance is immense; this bibliography includes mainly printed material published in the Western Hemisphere. Included is descriptive dance material found in books that recall early sojourns in the New World. These books, written by Europeans traveling or living in the Americas, document slaves' dances and festivals. Periodical articles are also included: reviews, interviews, and general articles on black dance. Books and articles in foreign languages appear when necessary. Much of the material on dance in Latin America, for example, appears only in Spanish or Portuguese.

Many citations to newspaper articles lack page numbers. These articles were located in the clipping files of the Schomburg Center for Research in Black Culture or the Dance Collection of the New York Public; library and page numbers are not noted on the clippings. Arrangement is alphabetical by author. Entries are briefly annotated unless their titles indicate their contents. Almost all the material was located at the New York Public Library, either at its General Research Division or Dance Collection, or at the Schomburg Center. All the material in the bibliography has been examined.

Following the bibliography is a subject index designed to be as specific as possible. While one can find general entries such as Jamaica or dancing, one can also find entries for specific dances, ceremonies, rites, or celebrations, such as "lindy hop," "John Canoe," and "Christmas."

The researcher should understand that this bibliography is by no means comprehensive, and errors, for which I take responsibility, may appear. I hope that it assists researchers in their quest for information on black dance.

BIBLIOGRAPHY

Contestants for the Cakewalk Crown   *Unknown*

Schomburg Center for Research in Black Culture
The New York Public Library
Astor, Lenox and Tilden Foundations

1. [A., R.E.] R.E.A. "Ballet with a Difference." *Evening Times* [Glasgow] (Sept. 10, 1957).

   Reviews the New York Negro Ballet in Glasgow.

2. Abdul, Raoul. "Lenwood Morris Mourned." *New York Amsterdam News* (Mar. 21, 1981).

3. Acquarone, Francisco. *História da Música Brasileira.* Rio de Janeiro, 1948.

   "Canticos e dansas afro-brasileiros," p. 122.

4. Adams, Alicia. "The Black Aesthetic and Dance, Part II—Black Forms and Dance." *The Feet* (June 1973): 28.

   The elements of black dance (African, jazz, tap, modern, and ballet) and how they are expressed by such choreographers as Alvin Ailey, Rod Rodgers, Eleo Pomare, and Arthur Mitchell.

5. ———. and Dedra Hurd. "Black Choreographers and Dancers Speak on the Value of Critics." *The Feet* (June 1973): 6-11.

6. Adams, Alicia. "Dance Theatre of Harlem." *The Feet* (June 1973): 12, 30.

7. "African Dancers and Singers Appear in Recital in Harlem." *New York Age* (Oct. 21, 1933).

   Reports on a program including works by Asadata Dafora.

8. "Africans." *The New Yorker* (May 19, 1934).

   Profiles Asadata Dafora and the composing of "Kykunkor."

9. Ahye, Molly. *Golden Heritage.* Petit Valley, Trinidad and Tobago: Heritage Cultures, Ltd., 1978.

   Describes the multi-ethnic dance heritage of Trinidad, including the French, Spanish, East Indian, and African legacies. The first chapter covers carnival and its character dances. Other chapters discuss funerary dances, reels and jigs, and social dances. The appendix lists the dances and the occasion when they are danced.

10.   Ailey, Alvin. "African Odyssey." *Dance Magazine* (May 1968): 50-53, 86-88.

Ailey chronicles the 1967 African tour of his company, the first American dance company to make a lengthy tour of Africa.

11.   "Ailey Gets Ford Funds." *Dance Herald* 1 (1975): 1.

12.   Alderham, Joseph. "Story of an Old-Timer." *Dance Magazine* 36 (Sept. 1962): 50-52.

A brief biography of white minstrel and eccentric dancer Joe Bennett acknowledging the black roots of minstrel and vaudeville dancing.

13.   Alegría, Ricardo E. "The Fiesta of Santiago Apostal (St. James the Apostle) in Loíza, Puerto Rico." *Journal of American Folklore* 69 (1956): 123-34.

Studies of Loíza as an example of the integration of Puerto Rican culture with the contribution of African culture. The Festival of Santiago Apostal is emphasized with detailed descriptions of the fiesta and its dances.

14.   Alexander, J.E. *Transatlantic Sketches, Comprising Visits to the Most Interesting Scenes in North and South America and the West Indies.* Philadelphia: Key and Biddle, 1833.

Describes a black holiday in Dutch Guiana (pp. 60-61), a Joan-Johnny dance in Barbados (p. 94), and a "quality ball" of black people.

15.   Alexander, Janice Berman. "Bettis: 'Streetcar' Vehicle for Expansion." *Newsday* (Jan. 14, 1982).

Valerie Bettis recalls her creation of *Streetcar Named Desire* and comments on Dance Theatre of Harlem's revival of it.

16. ——: "Dance Review: A Delightful 'Firebird Suite.'" *Newsday* (Jan. 14, 1982).

Dance Theatre of Harlem.

17. ——. "Dance Review: Harlem Troupe in 'Streetcar.'" *Newsday* (Jan. 16, 1982).

Dance Theatre of Harlem dances *Streetcar Named Desire*.

18. Alexander, Otis Douglas. *Black Experience and Influence in Dance*. N.p.: n.p., 1976.

A brief working bibliography to be used for the study of dance in the United States and the Caribbean.

19. Alladin, M.P. *Folk Dances of Trinidad and Tobago*. Maraval, Trinidad: n.p., 1974.

Identifies and describes the major folk dances of Trinidad. Gives the origins of the dances including the dances of carnival. Some of the dances discussed are bongo, calinda, shango (of African origin), the bélé and pique (of French with African influences).

20. Allen, Zita D. "'Let George Do It to It.' George Faison Universal Dance Experience." *Dance Magazine* (Apr. 1974): 26, 28, 31.

Reviews the George Faison Universal Dance Experience performing at Hunter College, Feb. 4-24, 1974.

21. ——. "Dancing in the Holes: Bernice Johnson Dance Company, Sounds in Motion." *Dance Magazine* (June 1974): 30, 32, 68.

22. ——. "Dance Theatre of Harlem—To Prove What???" *Dance Magazine* (July 1974): 21, 25-27.

Reviews the Dance Theatre of Harlem's first major season at the ANTA Theater, Apr. 20-28, 1974. Remarks on a *New York Times* caption in an article on DTH "to prove blacks can dance ballet" and reminds readers that several companies have gone before.

23.   ———. "Dance and Politics: Alvin Ailey Repertory Workshop; Shawneequa Baker Scott; Felice Lesser; Thomas Holt." *Dance Magazine* (Oct. 1975): 75-78.

24.   ———. "Majesty in Motion: Judith Jamison." *Encore American and Worldwide News* (Dec. 22, 1975): 26-28.

25.   ———. "Black Dance Doesn't Exist: Eleo Pomare Dance Company Choreomutations: George Faison Universal Dance Experience." *Dance Magazine* (May 1976): 110-12.

States that there is no black dance as such, meaning no one movement style that can be called black. There are only black choreographers whose work reflects their training, values, and individual personalities. The remaining part of the article contains reviews of performances by the companies mentioned in the title.

26.   ———. "Blacks and Ballet." *Dance Magazine* (July 1976): 65-70.

A historical overview of black participation in classical ballet from the 1920s to the Dance Theatre of Harlem era.

27.   ———. "Buffalo Black Dance: Full Emotional Spectrum." *New York Amsterdam News* (June 25, 1977): D-7.

Profiles this company of five women and its artistic director Carole Kariamu Welsh.

28.   ———. "Alvin Ailey, 20 Years on a Shoestring." *New York Amsterdam News* (Dec. 20, 1978): D-11.

Ailey speaks of his struggle to keep his company financially viable for 20 years.

29. ———. "Delacorte Dance Festival: Delicious." *New York Amsterdam News* (Sept. 15, 1979): 36.

Reviews performances by Buster Brown, Ernest Brown, Charles "Cookie" Cook, and Leslie "Bubba" Gaines of the Copasetics.

30. ———. "The Great American 'Black Dance' Mystery." *Freedomways* 20, no. 4 (1980): 283-90.

Attempts a definition of black dance by asking certain questions and discusses the white view of black dance, which the author feels oversimplifies and ignores a body of work.

31. ———. "An Interview with Pearl Primus." *New York Amsterdam News* (June 21, 1980): 36.

Primus on dance.

32. ———. "Anna Benna Sims: Toe-Dancing in the Big City." *Essence* (Aug. 1980): 12-13.

Anna Benna Sims was the first and, in 1980, the only black woman dancer with the American Ballet Theater.

33. ———. "Alvin Ailey Dancers: A Breed Apart." *New York Amsterdam News* (Dec. 20, 1980).

Highlights some of the Ailey company dancers. Mentions Donna Wood, Marilyn Banks, Sarita Allen, Maxine Sherman, Ulysses Dove, and Gary DeLoatch.

34. ———. "Dancemobile's Winter Series: Exciting Opening Weekend." *New York Amsterdam News* (Feb. 14, 1981).

Reviews the first weekend of a series at the Symphony Space, New York City. The groups performing: Rod Rodgers, Pearl Primus, Alvin Ailey Repertory Ensemble, Sounds in Motion, International Afrikan American Ballet, Philadanco, and Sombe Yembe Dancers.

35.   ———. "Dancemobile: Beautiful Funky Flippany." *New York Amsterdam News* (Feb. 21, 1981).

Reviews the second weekend of a series at the Symphony Space, New York City. The companies performing: Nanette Bearden Chamber Dance Company, La Rocque Bey's Dancers and Drummers, Al Perryman, Thomas Pinnock, Eleo Pomare, and Otis Sallid.

36.   ———. "Sara Yarborough: Something New Has Been Added." *New York Amsterdam News* (May 23, 1981): 36.

37.   ———. "Eleo Pomare Opens Dancemobile Summer Season." *New York Amsterdam News* (Aug. 8, 1981): 25.

Reviews performance of "Junkie" and Craig Moore's "Piece for Piano."

38.   ———. "Choreographer Billy Wilson, Exciting, Exciting Life." *New York Amsterdam News* (Sept. 26, 1981): 56.

Profiles Billy Wilson's career and choreographic style.

39.   ———. "How Many Dance Companies Fit in a Phone Booth?" *Village Voice* (Mar. 16, 1982): 82.

Reviews the opening of the Dancemobile winter series at the Symphony Space, New York City, Mar. 1982.

40.   ———. "BBBB." *Village Voice* (Oct. 28, 1982).

Reviews "Big Bold Black and in Brooklyn" at the Thelma Hill Performing Arts Center. The following groups performed: Mama Lu Parks Traditional Jazz Company, Detroit City Dance Company, Najwa Dance Corp., Philadanco, Newark Dance Company, and Garth Fagan's Bucket Dance Company.

41.   Almeida, Bira. *Capoeira; A Brazilian Art Form.* N.p: Sun Wave, Inc., 1981.

42. Almeida, Renato. *Danses Africaines en Amérique Latine.* Rio de Janeiro: MEC, Companha de Defesa Folclore Brasileiro, 1969.

Discusses popular Latin American dances and their roots in Africa and Afro-American cults. Some of the dances mentioned: the merengue, calenda, samba, tango, and the bossa nova. There is also a review of Afro-American dance scholarship covering Cuba, Brazil, and Haiti.

43. "Alvin Ailey." *Negro Digest* (Oct. 1962): 46-47.

44. *Alvin Ailey American Dance Theater.* New York: William Morrow, 1978.

The content is mainly photographs. The text introduces Ailey, gives biographical information, a history of his company, and describes twelve works.

45. "Alvin Ailey and Company." *Dance Magazine* (May 1958): 65-66.

46. "Alvin Ailey Dance Group to Australia." *New York Amsterdam News* (Jan. 13, 1962): 16.

47. "Alvin Ailey Dancers Thrill." *New York Amsterdam News* (Feb. 27, 1960): 13.

Reviews a performance at the Harlem Y. Performed "Blues Suite," "Mean Old Firseo," and "Jack O'Diamond."

48. "Alvin Ailey Is Spingarn Medalist." *Michigan Chronicle* (Jan. 8, 1977): C-8.

49. "Alvin Ailey Talks to *Dance and Dancers* : An Interview." *Dance and Dancers* (Apr. 1965): 32.

50. "Ambassador Destiné to Spend Christmas under Voodoo Tonnelles." *Haiti Sun* (Dec. 16, 1956).

Jean-Léon Destiné.

51. "American Juvenile Star Shows English Theatregoers How Real Dancing Is Done." *Chicago Defender* (Aug. 15, 1936).

Features Harold Nicholas of the Nicholas Brothers.

52. "American Negro Ballet." *New Yorker* (Dec. 4, 1937).

Reviews the company debut.

53. Anderson, Eva. "The Baltimore Dance Theatre." *The Western Journal of Black Studies* (Summer 1981): 116-17.

54. Anderson, Jack. "Chuck Davis Dance Company, Clark Center, N.Y.C., February 10, 11, 12, 1973." *Dance Magazine* 47 (Apr. 1973): 90-92.

Reviews "Chronology of Black Heritage," a trilogy presented on three nights.

55. ――――. "Alpha Omega 1-7 Theatrical Dance Company; Negro Ensemble Company Dance and Music Festival, St. Mark's Playhouse, N.Y.C., April 3, 1973." *Dance Magazine* 47 (June 1973): 68-69.

56. ――――. "Black Dance Workshop of Buffalo; Negro Ensemble Company Dance and Music Festival. St. Mark's Playhouse, N.Y.C., March 31, 1973." *Dance Magazine* 47 (June 1973): 68

57. ――――. Dance: Trio by the Ailey." *New York Times* (May 8, 1978): C19.

Reviews "Masakela Language," Louis Falco's "Caravan," and "Pas de Duke."

58. ――――. "Dance: Solos by the Ailey." *New York Times* (May 18, 1978).

Reviews the Alvin Ailey American Dance Theater at the City Center, New York City. The works performed: "Journey" (Joyce Trisler), "Hermit Songs" (Ailey), "Lark Ascending," "Gazelle," and "Night Creatures."

59. ——. "Dance: Pearl Primus Presents 'Earth Theater.'" *New York Times* (Aug. 21, 1979).

Reviews a performance of the Pearl Primus-Percival Borde Dance Company at the Perry St. Theater, New York City.

60. ——. "Charles Moore Group and Drums of Africa." *New York Times* (Sept. 30, 1979): 53.

Reviews a performance at Marymount Manhattan Theater, Sept. 28, 1979.

61. ——. "Dance: Philadanco Troupe in Central Park Festival." *New York Times* (Sept. 11, 1980).

62. ——. "Dance: Theater of Harlem Troupe." *New York Times* (Jan. 12, 1981).

Reviews Dance Theatre of Harlem's performance of "Four Temperaments," "Manifestations," and "Scheherezade."

63. ——. "Dance: Harlem Troupe in 'Serenade.'" *New York Times* (Jan. 19, 1981).

Reviews the Dance Theatre of Harlem performing "Serenade," "Mirage," "Doina," and "Le Corsaire Pas de Deux."

64. ——. "Dance: The Primus 'Earth.'" *New York Times* (Mar. 25, 1981).
This performance of the "Earth Theater" at the Theater of the Riverside Church was dedicated to the late Percival Borde and Alphonse Cimber.

65. ——. "Black Dance: Saluting the Classics." *New York Times* (Sept. 19, 1981): 11.

Reviews the Negro Ensemble Company's "A Salute to the Black Classics of Dance."

66. ———. "The Dance: An Evening with Von Grona." *New York Times* (Dec. 10, 1981).

Reviews the revival of the First American Negro Ballet performing at Riverside Church.

67. ———. "Dance: Harlem Troupe Offers 'Equus' as Ballet." *New York Times* (Jan. 25, 1982).

Reviews the première of Dance Theatre of Harlem's *Equus*.

68. ———. "Dancemobile Rolls in for Black Dance Series." *New York Times* (Feb. 5, 1982).

69. ———. "Dance: Danz, Inc. a New Company." *New York Times* (Feb. 14, 1982).

Reviews a performance given at the Symphony Space as part of the Dancemobile winter series of 1982.

70. Anderson, John. "Kykunkor." *New York Evening Journal* (June 4, 1934).

71. Anderson, John Q. "The New Orleans Voodoo Ritual Dance and Its Twentieth Century Survivals." *Southern Folklore Quarterly* 24 (June 1960): 135-43.

Tracing the American popular dance, the author asserts that the strongest force in the development of American social dance is the ritual dance of the voodoo cult. He describes the ritual dance and other dances such as the calinda and their similarities to such dances as the lindy hop, charleston, jitterbug, Suzie Q., etc.

72. Andrade, Mario de. "Os Congos." *Lanterna Verde* (Feb. 1935): 36-53.

73. ———. "O Samba Rural Paulista." *Revista do Arquivo Municipal* (São Paulo) 4, no. 41 (1937): 37-116.

    Describes the African influences in the dances performed during the annual Pirapora festival in São Paulo, Brazil.

74. ———. "As Danças Dramáticas do Brasil." *Boletin Latino Americano de Música* 6 (Apr. 1946): 49-97.

75. ———. *Danças Dramáticas do Brasil.* São Paulo: Livraria Martins Editôra, 1959.

76. "Andre Drew School of the Dance." *Ebony* (June 1956): 27-30.

    Ex-Dunham dancer operates studio with an interracial staff in Philadelphia.

77. Andrews, George Reid. *The Afro-Argentines of Buenos Aires, 1800-1900.* Madison: University of Wisconsin Press, 1980.

    Chapter 9 surveys Afro-Argentine participation in and contribution to the cultural life of Buenos Aires. Discusses condombes, the milonga, and the history of the tango.

78. "Another Dancing De Lavallade." *Hue* (Sept. 1956): 43-47.

    Yvonne De Lavallade, Carmen's sister, makes a name for herself.

79. "Another First." *New York Amsterdam News* (Oct. 6, 1951): 1

    Announces the signing of Janet Collins for the Metropolitan Opera Ballet.

80. Anthony, Bill. "Soul at the Center, Alice Tully Hall, July 31, 1972." *Dance Magazine* (Oct. 1972): 84, 86.

    Reviews works by George Faison, Diane Ramos, Eleo Pomare, and Rod Rodgers.

81. Apel, Paul Hermann. *Music of the Americas, North and South.*
     New York: Vantage, 1958.

     Has very brief descriptions of some black dances and rhythms
     in North, Central, and South America.

82. Araujo, Alceu Maynard. "Jongo." *Revista do Arquivo Municipal*
     [São Paulo] 128 (Oct. 1949): 45-54.

     Describes a Brazilian dance of Angolan origin in which men
     and women participate.

83. Arauz, Reina Torres de. "La Danza de los Cuenecue: Folklore
     Afro-Americano en Azuero." ("The Dance of the Cuenecue:
     Afro-Panamanian Folklore.") In *Actas del 1 Congreso
     International de Folklorologia.* Guarare—Provincia de los
     Santos, Panama: n.p., 33-42.

84. "Are Night Club Dancers Getting Younger?" *Jet* (Dec. 18, 1954):
     60-62.

85. Armstrong, Jocklyn. "The Fred Benjamin Dance Company, the
     Cubiculo January 20, 1970." *Dance Magazine* 44 (Mar.
     1970): 90.

86. Armstrong, Orland Kay. *Old Massa's People: The Old Slaves Tell
     Their Story.* Indianapolis: Bobbs-Merrill, 1931.

     Former slaves recount their lives in slavery. Chapter 10, "Gay
     Times," describes celebrations, amusements, and quadroon balls.
     Chapter 20, "Conjur Stuff," describes a New Orleans voodoo
     ceremony with dancing.

87. Aronson, Kristin. "New Joffrey Dance Program Mixed Bag."
     Newsworld (Nov. 17, 1978).

     This review briefly mentions Christian Holder.

88. Asbury, Herbert. *The French Quarter: An Informal History of the
     New Orleans Underworld.* New York: Pocket Books, 1949.

Describes dancing in Place Congo (pp. 176-87) and quadroon balls (pp. 92-95).

89. Aschenbrenner, Joyce. *Katherine Dunham: Reflections on the Social and Political Contexts of Afro-American Dance.* New York: CORD, Inc., 1981.

Also includes notations of the Dunham method and techniques by Lavinia Williams.

90. "Aspirant to Pulpit Detoured Draws Job as 'Sportin' Life.'" *New York Herald Tribune* (Mar. 15, 1942).

Profiles Avon Long.

91. Assuncão, Fernando. "Aportaciones Para un Estudio Sobre los Orígenes de la Zamacueca (Baile Popular Hispanoamericano de las Regiones Costeras de Pacifico)." *Folklore Americano* 17-18, no. 16 (1969-70): 5-39.

Surveys the African influence in the New World with emphasis on the zamacueca dance of Peru.

92. "Au Revoir to Dafora." *New York Times* (May 22, 1960).

Reports that Asadata Dafora sailed to Sierra Leone to become its first cultural director upon independence.

93. Austin, Mary. "Buck and Wing and Bill Robinson." *The Nation* (Apr. 28, 1926): 476.

Discusses what inspires Bill Robinson.

94. Avery, Verna. "Negro Dance and Its Influence on Negro Music." In *Black Music in Our Culture: Curricular Ideas on the Subjects, Materials and Problems* edited by Dominique-René de Lerma, 79-92. Kent, Ohio: Kent State University Press, 1970.

Discusses the African influences on the dances of South America, the Caribbean, and the United States. Describes certain dances such as the cakewalk, tap dance, samba, and batucada.

95. Ayers, Tomi. "17-year-old 'Salome' Captivates Los Angeles Dance Enthusiasts." *Chicago Defender* (Apr. 29, 1950): 14.

Reviews Carmen De Lavallade's debut performance with the Dance Theatre in Los Angeles featuring the choreography of Lester Horton.

96. [B.,H.] H.B. "Alvin Ailey, Ernest Parham and Companies." *Dance Observer* (June-July 1958).

Ailey performs at the 92nd St. Y., Mar. 30,1958.

97. ———. "Walter Nicks and Nino Banome." *Dance Observer* 28, no. 3 (Mar. 1961): 44.

Reviews Walter Nicks and his company at the 92nd St. Y., New York City, Jan. 15, 1961.

98. "Baby Lawrence Jazz Tap Percussionist Buried in N.J." *New York Amsterdam News* (Apr. 13, 1974): C-3.

99. Bailey, A. Peter. "Nana Yao Opare Dinizulu." *Caribe* 7 (nos. 1-2): 13-14.

100. ———. "Rapping with Marie Brooks." *Black Theater Alliance Newsletter* 4, no. 12 (Dec. 1979): 1, 4.

In this interview the founder of the Marie Brooks Children's Dance Research Theatre talks of her career and her methods of training young people.

101. ———. "Rapping with Joan Meyers Brown." *Black Theater Alliance Newsletter* 5, no. 8 (Aug. 1980): 1.

Interviews the founder of Philadanco.

102. Bailey, Bill. "Why I'm Dancing Again." *Negro Digest* (Sept. 1951): 8-13.

103. Baker, Robb. "Black Dance in the Seventies: Two Directions." *After Dark* (Feb. 1974).

In the first part Arthur Hall states that "blacks must get back to their heritage, their tradition, the dance and culture of Africa itself." In the second part Alvin Ailey states that his is a company "that makes a connection with the American dance past and future, and, very strongly, with the black past and future."

104. ———. "New Dance." *Dance Magazine* (Nov. 1974): 84-85.

Reviews the Alvin Ailey American Dance Theater at the New York State Theater, Aug. 1974.

105. ———. "Alvin Ailey's Surprises." *New York Daily News* (May 5, 1983).

Reviews the opening of Alvin Ailey's company at New York's City Center. The works performed: "Seven Journeys" (a première), "Pigs and Fishes," "Satyriade," and "The Stack Up."

106. Balcom, Lois. "What Chance Has the Negro Dancer?" *Dance Observer* (Nov. 1944): 110-11.

Criticizing an early Pearl Primus performance, the author comments on the different aspects of her dancing: "Negro" and "modern." The author anticipates that Primus will develop further.

107. ———. "The Negro Dances Himself." *Dance Observer* (Dec. 1944): 122-24.

Discusses audience expectations and assumptions when watching black dancers. The author also states, when referring to Pearl Primus, that only when she is truest to herself will she say what she can in modern terms.

108.   Ballard, Delores. "'Fat Tuesday' Offers Different Entertainment."
           Jackson Sun [Jackson, Tenn.] (Feb. 17, 1977).

           Reviews Arthur Hall's Afro-American Dance Ensemble.

109.   "Ballerina De Lavallade." *Our World* (July 1953): 49-50.

110.   "Ballet: Afro-American Dance Featured." *Berkshire Eagle
           Summer Magazine* (Aug. 9-Aug. 17, 1969).

           A brief history of the Afro-American Dance Ensemble and an
           interview with founder Arthur Hall.

111.   "Ballet Beauties." *Hue* (Dec. 1957): 24-26.

           Photo article pictures young ballerinas from around the United
           States.

112.   "Ballet Beauty to Seek Dance Fame in U.S." *Jet* (July 1, 1953):
           34-35.

           Evelyn Andrade, Jamaican-born ballet dancer, to attempt a
           career with Katherine Dunham.

113.   "Ballet Negres." *Dancing Times* (Sept. 19, 1952).

           Announces a forthcoming London season of this British black
           company.

114.   "Ballet Star; Arthur Mitchell Is One of the Top Soloists with
           World-Famous New York City Company." *Ebony* (Nov.
           1959): 122-24, 126.

115.   "The Bandits' Beach Ballet." *Hue* (Jan. 1957): 56-59.

           Night club dancers Norma Washington and Frances Neely bill
           themselves as "The Bandits" and pack them in.

116.   Banes, Sally. "Wedding Day Blues." *Soho Weekly News* (Sept.
           6, 1979).

Review of Pearl Primus-Percival Borde Dance Company's "Earth Theater" at the Perry St. Theater, New York City.

117. Banting, John. "The Dancing of Harlem." In *Negro Anthology, 1931-1933* edited by Nancy Cunard, 322-23. London: Wishart, 1934.

Enumerates the popular dances of the time.

118. Barnes, Clive and Peter Williams. "Transatlantic Return." *Dance and Dancers* 12, no. 10 (Oct. 1961): 9-16.

Reviews all aspects of Ballet: USA's second visit to London. John Jones is reviewed in "Afternoon of a Faun" and "Events."

119. Barnes, Clive. "Dancing Inspires Twenty-Two Negro Youths." *New York Times* (May 13, 1966).

The founding, purpose, and results of the Ron Davis Dancers.

120. ———. "Dance: The Remarkable Don Redlich at Henry Street." *New York Times* (Oct. 17, 1966).

Dual review includes Eleo Pomare performing at the 92nd St. Y.

121. ———. "Dance: Bill Frank as Choreographer." *New York Times* (Nov. 13, 1966).

122. ———. "Dance: A McKayle Debut." *New York Times* (Feb. 9, 1967).

Review of a performance of "Black New World" at the 92nd St. Y. in New York City.

123. ———. "Dance: An Evenly Textured Program." *New York Times* (Jan. 23, 1968).

Reviews the Donald McKayle Dance Company at the Brooklyn Academy of Music.

124.   ———. "As Long as They Have Talent." *New York Times* (Apr. 14, 1968).

Summarizes black activity in dance and looks at the question, "Does equal opportunity exist in the dance world?"

125.   ———. "Dance: Beatty Winding Up the City Center Season." *New York Times* (May 21, 1969).

Reviews the Talley Beatty Company in the American Dance Season.

126.   ———. "Shaping a Black Classic Ballet." *New York Times* (Oct. 12, 1969).

Notes the founding of the Dance Theatre of Harlem and the expansion of blacks into classical ballet.

127.   ———. "Dance: Unfinished 'River.'" *New York Times* (June 26, 1970).

Reviews the American Ballet Theater's "River" choreographed by Alvin Ailey to music by Duke Ellington.

128.   ———. "Lovely Dancers—Black, White or Green." *New York Times* (Jan. 24, 1971).

Arthur Mitchell and the Dance Theatre of Harlem.

129.   ———. "Dance: Delacorte's First of Two 'Rain' Specials." *New York Times* (Sept. 17, 1971).

Reviews the George Faison Universal Dance Experience and the Interboro Dance Company.

130.   ———. "Dance Marathon Setting Fast Pace." *New York Times* (Oct. 17, 1972).

Reviews the première of "Sojourn" by Donald McKayle and his Inner City Repertory Dance Company.

131. ———. "Dance: Ailey Performs for Its Life." *New York Times* (Nov. 30, 1973).

Reviews gala benefit for the Alvin Ailey company.

132. ———. "Dance: Missa Brevis." *New York Times* (Dec. 6, 1973).

Reviews a performance of José Limon's work added to the Ailey repertoire.

133. ———. "Dance: Classic Ballet, Black Insights." *New York Times* (Apr. 14, 1974).

Reviews the second program of Dance Theatre of Harlem's first Broadway season at the ANTA Theater. The works performed: Arthur Mitchell's "Holberg Suite" and "Biosfera," Talley Beatty's "Caravansera," and Louis Johnson's "Forces of Rhythm."

134. ———. "Dance Theatre of Harlem at Home on Broadway." *New York Times* (Apr. 18, 1974).

Reviews the first performance of the Dance Theatre of Harlem's first season at the ANTA Theater. The works performed: Louis Johnson's "Wings," Geoffrey Holder's "Dougla," and Arthur Mitchell's "Fête Noire," as well as "Le Corsaire Pas de Deux."

135. ———. "The Ailey Steps Up to Lincoln Center." *New York Times* (Aug. 15, 1974).

Reviews the first night program at the New York State Theater.

136. ———. "Choreographers Cast Their Spell over Broadway." *New York Times* (Apr. 11, 1976).

Briefly mentions Geoffrey Holder in a general article on the dominance of dancing in Broadway musicals.

137. ———. "Donald McKayle's Latest Dance in Première." *New York Times* (Dec. 11, 1976).

Reviews McKayle's "Blood Memories" as danced by the Alvin Ailey American Dance Theater.

138. ———. "Dance: à la Jazz." *New York Times* (July 24, 1977).

Reviews Pepsi Bethel and his Authentic Jazz Theater.

139. ———. "Harlem Dance Opens with 'Swan Lake.'" *New York Post* (Jan. 10, 1980): 28.

Reviews the opening of Dance Theatre of Harlem's three-week season at New York's City Center. The works performed: "Swan Lake" Act II, "Paquita," Glen Tetley's "Greening," "Le Corsaire Pas de Deux," and "Dougla."

140. ———. "'Paquita' Première by Harlem Dance." *New York Post* (Jan. 12, 1980).

Dance Theatre of Harlem.

141. ———. "Harlem Dance Emerging as 'Big League Contender.'" *New York Post* (Jan. 16, 1980).

States that the Dance Theatre of Harlem has developed its classical style to such a degree as to be considered in the same league as the New York City Ballet, American Ballet Theater, and the Joffrey Ballet.

142. ———. "Joyous Dancing Refreshing." *New York Post* (Sept. 17, 1981): 28.

Reviews an Alvin Ailey Repertory Ensemble performance at the Riverside Dance Festival, Sept. 16, 1981.

143. ———. "Harlem Dances from the Heart." *New York Post* (Jan. 26, 1982).

Gives an overview of Dance Theatre of Harlem's repertory during its season at City Center.

144. ———. "Harlem's Frankly Good 'Frankie and Johnny.'" *New York Post* (Jan. 28, 1982).

Dance Theatre of Harlem.

145. Barnick, Kaye. "Debbie Allen Triple-Threat in the Theatre." *Sepia* (Mar. 1978): 39-46.

146. "Baron's Caribbean Carnival." *Life* (Mar. 3, 1961).

Picture of a socialite's Caribbean party; features a limbo dancer.

147. Barthel, Joan. "When You Dream, Dream Big." *New York Times* (Aug. 18, 1968): Section 2, p. 1.

Arthur Mitchell's career and his time with the Harlem School of the Arts prior to the formation of the Dance Theatre of Harlem.

148. Bartlett, B.K.S. "Talley Beatty Company in Vivid Performance at John Hancock Hall." *Boston Globe* (Jan. 15, 1952).

149. Barton, Peter. *Staying Power: Performing Artists Talk about Their Lives/Interviews and Photos*. New York: Dial Press, 1980.

Features Ulysses Dove of the Alvin Ailey American Dance Theater (pp. 126-37).

150. Barzel, Ann. "Nina Novak's 'Giselle' Role Challenges Reign of Alicias." *Chicago American* (Apr. 11, 1958): 13.

This review of a Ballet Russe de Monte Carlo performance mentions Raven Wilkinson.

151. "Bassa Moona." *Dance Observer* (Oct. 1939).

Reviews the production done under the auspices of the WPA Federal Theater Project.

152. Bassett, A.L. "Going to Housekeeping in North Carolina."
Lippincott's Magazine 28 (1881): 205-08.

Discusses the manners and customs of the southern black with
a brief explanation of the cakewalk.

153. Bastide, Roger. "Les Filles des Dieux de Bahia." *Le Revue de
Paris* 60, no. 1 (Jan. 1953): 124-30.

154. Battey, Jean. "Capitol Ballet Performs Brightly." *Washington
Post* (June 1, 1968).

Reviews the Capitol Ballet Company of Washington, D.C.

155. Bauzo, Luis F. "Kubata: Cuban Cultural Authenticity in Music
and Dance." *Caribe* 7, nos. I & II: 36-38.

Profiles Kubata, an Afro-Cuban dance group in New York City
that preserves and revitalizes traditional forms of Cuban dance as
manifested in the Lucumi cult, secret societies, and popular secular
dances such as the rumba.

156. Baxter, Ivy. *The Arts of an Island: The Development of the
Culture and of the Folk and Creative Arts in Jamaica, 1494-
1962 (Independence)*. Metuchen, N.J.: Scarecrow Press,
1970.

Surveys the folk art of Jamaica. The pertinent chapters are
"The John Canoe Masquerade," "Social Dances and Dance Steps,"
and "Religious Cult Survivals as Revealed through Dance and
Song."

157. Baxter, Robert. "Begging Money to Support a Young Black
Dance Troupe." *Courier-Post* [Cherry Hill, N.J.] (July 29,
1978): 34.

Discusses Philadanco's fund-raising problems.

158. Baymiller, Joanna. "Harlem Ensemble Takes from History." *Minneapolis Star* (May 5, 1981).

Reviews a performance of the Dance Theatre of Harlem at the Minneapolis Northrup Auditorium. The works performed: "Four Temperaments," "Serenade," "Le Corsaire," "Scheherazade," and "Manifestations."

159. "Be Bop Dance Craze Sweeps Nation." *Color* (Aug. 1949): 14-16.

160. Beaufort, John. "Broadway's Bubbling Black Musicals." *Christian Science Monitor* (Sept. 9, 1976), 22.

161. ———. "Black Broadway." *Christian Science Monitor* (May 7, 1980).

Reviews the revue with performances by Gregory Hines, Charles "Cookie" Cook, Leslie "Bubba" Gaines, and John W. Bubbles.

162. "Beauty in Motion." *Our World* (May 1955): 64-66.

Carmen De Lavallade.

163. "Because I Love My People." *Success Unlimited* (Mar. 1958): 4-6.

Interviews Lavinia Williams.

164. Beckford, Ruth. *Katherine Dunham: A Biography.* New York: Marcel Dekker, Inc., 1979.

165. Beckwith, Martha Warren. *Black Roadways: A Study of Jamaican Folk Life.* Chapel Hill, N.C.: University of North Carolina Press, 1929.

166. Becraft, Gina. "Ben Vereen Still Improving with Age." *Newsworld* (June 10, 1979).

167. Behague, Gerard. "Book Review: Ortiz Oderigo, Nestor. *Calunga, Croquis del Candombe.* Buenos Aires: Editorial Universitaria de Buenos Aires, 1969." *Ethnomusicology* 15, no. 2 (May 1971): 284-86.

168. Beiswanger, George. "Broadway on Its Toes." *Theatre Arts* (Feb. 1940): 107-18.

Reviews dance in Broadway's musical comedies. There is a brief mention of "Swingin' the Dream" in which "perfectly swell dancers from Harlem were wasted on bad chores."

169. ———. "Broadway Steps Out." *Theatre Arts* (Jan. 1941): 32-39.

An overview of dance in Broadway musicals of 1940-41 with a brief critique of "Cabin in the Sky," with choreography by Katherine Dunham.

170. ———. "Womanly, Black, Freed, Spelman Dancer Debuts." *Atlanta Journal* (Jan. 24, 1971).

Reviews a performance of Diana Ramos at the Spelman College Fine Arts Auditorium.

171. Beliz, Anel E. "Los Congos: Afro-Panamanian Dance Drama." *Américas* 11, no. 11 (Nov. 1959): 31-33.

Describes the characters and dances of this Panamanian dance-drama portraying a slave uprising.

172. Bell, Hesketh J. *Obeah: Witchcraft in the West Indies.* London: Low, Marston & Co., 1893.

Along with a description of obeah there are chapters on dancing, Anansi, weddings, ghost-lore, and Christmas celebrations. Chapter 3 describes dances such as the calinda and belair.

173. Benjamin, Roberto. "Congos da Paraíba." *Cadernos de Folclore,* N.S. 18 (Aug. 1977): 3-23.

174. Bennett, Paul. "Philadanco Could've Danced All Night at University City H.S." *Philadelphia Tribune* (May 5, 1973).

175. Benson, Mae. "Broadway's Unheralded Maker of Big Stars." *Norfolk Journal and Guide* (Sept. 19, 1931).

Profiles Billy Pierce, dance teacher to the Broadway stars.

176. Berry, Abner W. "He Made Music with His Feet." *The Worker* (Dec. 11, 1949).

Bill Robinson.

177. Bettelheim, Judith. "Jamaican Jonkonnu and Related Caribbean Festivals." In *Africa and the Caribbean: The Legacies of a Link* edited by Margaret E. Crahan and Franklin W. Knight, 80-100. Baltimore and London: The Johns Hopkins University Press, 1979.

Includes junkanoo of Nassau and gombey of Bermuda.

178. "Betty Brisbane." *Sepia Record* (July 1954): 32-35.

179. Bezjak, Maja. "U Vrtlogu Ritma i Plesa." *Vjesnik* [Zagreb] (Oct. 29, 1980): 7.

Reviews the Chuck Davis Dance Company.

180. Biblioteca de Cultura Universitaria. *Panorama del Folklore Venezolano*. Caracas: Universidad Central, 1959.

Leading Venezuelan folklorists' essays on general topics, including dance.

181. "Bill Bailey, Dancing Preacher, Fights Satan with His Feet." *Sepia* (Dec. 1954): 26-28.

182. "Bill 'Bojangles' Robinson." *Vanity Fair* (June 1935).

183. "Bill (Bojangles) Robinson Says Negro Actor Is Being
      Emancipated." *New York Age* (Aug. 18, 1928).

184. "Bill Robinson Arraigned, Taps His Way Out of Court." *New
      York Post* (May 20, 1939).

      Robinson was arrested for obstructing traffic while looking at a
      theater marquee.

185. "Bill Robinson at 57, World's Greatest Tap Dancer." *Daily
      Gleaner* [Jamaica] (Dec. 7, 1935).

186. "Bill Robinson Funeral Cortege to Get Times Square Tribute."
      New York Herald Tribune (Nov. 27, 1949).

187. "Bill Robinson Is Dead at 71." *New York Sun* (Nov. 26, 1949).

188. "Bill Robinson Tells Some Dance Secrets." *New York Amsterdam
      News* (Dec. 10, 1930).

189. "Bill Robinson's Estate." *New York Times* (June 19, 1953).

190. "Bill Robinson's Estate Valued at Only $31.50." *New York Times*
      (Apr. 15, 1950).

191. "Billy Bailey Comes Home." *New York Sunday News* (July 29,
      1951).

      Bailey returns to dancing after preaching for several years.

192. "Billy Farrell, King of Cakewalkers, Ends 33-Year Odyssey and
      Comes Home." *New York Amsterdam News* (Aug. 11,
      1934).

      Sketches Billy Farrell's career from the time he won the
      cakewalk championship in 1895 at Madison Square Garden
      through his performances in vaudeville and minstrel shows.

193. "Billy Pierce, Noted Dancing Instructor Dies in New York."
      Washington Tribune (Apr. 21, 1933).

194. Biondo, Anne Marie. "Edna Guy McCully Leaves Inspired Legacy." *Fort Worth Star-Telegram* (Apr. 29, 1983).

Obituary profiles Edna Guy, an early concert dancer whose career was shortened by bad health.

195. Birnie, William A.H. "'Boom-Boom' Go the Drums as Giant Blacks Rehearse Jungle Play in WPA Project." *New York World-Telegram* (Aug. 28, 1936).

196. ———. "Birthdays Mean Little to Bill Robinson, 60." *New York World-Telegram* (Apr. 9, 1938).

197. Bishop, Nancy. "Brooklyn's Ben Vereen Recalls His Roots." *Staten Island Advance* (May 22, 1983).

198. "Black, Black." *Time* (Nov. 29, 1937).

Reviews the American Negro Ballet.

199. "Black Bottom to Bop." *Hue* (Jan. 1955): 60-63.

Al Minns and Leon James, former Savoy Ballroom dancers, illustrate old popular dances in their "Illustrated Jazz Lectures." Photos of the black bottom and Suzy Q., among others.

200. "Black Choreographers." *New York Times* (Jan. 16, 1967).

Reviews the first performances of the Association of Black Choreographers' workshop group.

201. "Black Dance Directory." *Dance Herald* 1, no. 1 (1975); 4, no. 2 (1975): 5.

Names and addresses of choreographers and companies located mainly in New York City.

202. "Black Dancers Bargain for Business Beat." *Black Enterprise* 4 (Aug. 1973): 38-41.

Discusses the financial facts of life faced by black dance companies in getting funding and support. Examines Alvin Ailey City Center Dance Theatre, Rod Rodgers Dance Company, and Tanawa Company.

203. "Black Dancers from Performing Arts School Achieve 'Fame.'" *Sepia* (Feb. 1981): 63-67.

Relates the story of fifteen black graduates of New York's High School of Performing Arts including Claude Thompson, Michael Peters, Ben Vereen, Altovise Davis, and Diane Day.

204. Black, Elizabeth. "A Show at the Quarter." *Theatre Arts Monthly* 16 (June 1932): 493-500.

Reminiscences of plantation entertainment by blacks, including dancing and caricaturing of ballroom dancing.

205. "Black Is Different." *Newsweek* (Dec. 7, 1981).

Brief article on Gregory Hines's life as a performer.

206. "Black Man Stars in Ballet." *Black America* 1, no. 4 (June 1970): 52-54.

Briefly describes the career of Arthur Mitchell and his work with the Dance Theatre of Harlem.

207. Blasis, Charles. *Traite Elementaire, Théorique et Pratique de l'Art de la Danse.* Milan: J. Beati et A. Tenenti, 1820. Translated by Mary Stewart Evens as *An Elementary Treatise upon the Theory and Practice of the Art of Dancing,* by Carlo Blasis.

Includes a chapter on black dancing in North and South America.

208. Blassingame, John W. *The Slave Community.* New York: Oxford University Press, 1972.

Describes slave life, the slave's heritage, culture, behavior, and personality. Chapter 1, "Enslavement, Acculturation, and African Survivals," has a good description of African dancing, slave funeral rites, the ring shout (pp. 65-66), and patting juba (p. 55).

209. Blesh, Rudi and Harriet Janis. *They All Played Ragtime.* New York: Knopf, 1950.

A history of ragtime that discusses the following: dancing in the Place Congo (pp. 81-84); the counjaille (p. 84); the cakewalk (pp. 96-100); rag dance (pp. 103-04); and ring shouts and rent shouts (pp. 184-209).

210. Bloomfield, Arthur. "Negro Ballet Rewarding." *San Francisco Call-Bulletin* (Aug. 16, 1952).

Reviews a performance of the Hollywood Negro Ballet in San Francisco's Marines' Memorial Theater.

211. Boas, Franziska. "Negro and the Dance as an Art." *Phylon* 10, no. 1 (1949): 38-42.

States that the black dancer's conception of dance is at the folk dance level and does not understand esthetic principles. Calls for support of those blacks who want to work creatively and develop into artists. Recommends that blacks study body movement and dance compositions instead of depending on showmanship and startling technique.

212. "Boatright Conquers Classical Bias." *New York Amsterdam News* (July 30, 1979): 31.

Charles Boatright has lead in Stuttgart Ballet's *Romeo and Juliet.*

213. "Bob Destine Has Been Signed for Fox's South Pacific Film." *Chicago Defender* (Dec. 1957): 19.

214.   Bohen, Tullia. "Thompson Troupe Shows Great Potential."
        Staten Island Advance (May 24, 1982).

        Reviews the second appearance of the Clive Thompson Dance
Company.

215.   ———. "Thompson Company Self-Assured in World Debut."
        Staten Island Advance (Aug. 25, 1982).

        Reviews the official debut of the Clive Thompson Dance
Company at Jacob's Pillow Dance Festival on Aug. 24, 1982.

216.   "Bojangles Free with a Caution." *New York Sun* (May 20,
        1939).

        Standing too long admiring a theater marquee with his name on
it, Bill Robinson is arrested for obstructing traffic on Broadway.

217.   "Bojangles Frees Georgia Fugitive." *New York World-Telegram*
        (Feb. 7, 1941).

        Bill Robinson posts bail for fugitive.

218.   "'Bojangles' Owed $60,000." *New York Journal-American* (June
        18, 1953).

219.   "Bojangles the Runner." *Chicago Defender* (Sept. 25, 1926).

220.   "'Bojangles' Wins Hat Dancing for Solid Hour." *Pittsburgh
        Courier* (July 6, 1935).

221.   Bond, Frederick W. *The Negro and the Drama.* Washington,
        D.C.: Associated Publishers, 1940. Reprint. Washington,
        D.C.: McGrath Publishing Company, 1969.

        Chapter 9, "Dance and Jazz," states that American dance has
been influenced by blacks. Bond describes the origins of various
American pop dances.

222. Borek, Tom. "Chuck Davis Dance Company, The Cubiculo N.Y.C., Feb. 9, 1971." *Dance Magazine* (Apr. 1971): 96.

     Review.

223. ———. "Festival of Black Dance; Manhattan Theater Club, N.Y.C. July 20-August 24, 1971." *Dance Magazine* (Oct. 1971): 89-90, 92.

     Review.

224. "Born to Dance." *Our World* (Jan. 1951): 19-21.

     Profiles Lavinia Williams's life as a dance teacher working from her basement studio after giving up her career for marriage and family.

225. "Born to Dance." *Ebony* (June 1955): 83-86.

     Pat Sides is successful as a night club dancer.

226. "Bossa Nova." *Ebony* (Mar. 1963): 103-06.

227. "Boston Ballet's Only Black Dancer Quits, Charging Bias." *Afro-American* (June 13, 1981): 6.

     Augustus Van Heerden, a native of South Africa, feels he has been unfairly passed over for important parts.

228. Bottaro, Marcellino. "Rituals and Candombés." In *Negro Anthology, 1931-1933* edited by Nancy Cunard, 317-20. London: Wishart, 1934.

229. Bourguignon, Erika E. "Trance Dance." *Dance Perspectives* 35 (Autumn 1968): 1-61.

     Discusses visionary and possessional dancing among Trinidad's Spiritual Baptists, St. Vincent's Shakers, Haiti's Voodoo, Brazil's Umbanda, and their African counterparts.

230. Bowen, Elbert R. "Negro Minstrels in Early Rural Missouri."
        Missouri Historical Review 47 (Jan. 1953): 103-09.

        Brief historical overview of minstrelsy and its success in rural
        Missouri.

231. Bowers, Theresa. "Alvin Ailey American Dance Theatre (in its
        Twentieth Anniversary Season, City Center New York).
        Katherine Dunham Gala (Carnegie Hall, Jan. 15, 1979)."
        Dance Magazine (May 1979): 44-49.

        Reviews two performances and opens with discussion of the
        question, "Is there any such thing as black dance?"

232. Brandon, Ivan. "Strives to Preserve Black Dance History." *The
        Daily News* [St. Thomas, V.I.] (Aug. 18, 1975).

        Profiles Joe Nash and his efforts to document the history of
        black dance.

233. Brathwaite, P.A., comp. and Serena U. Brathwaite, ed. *Musical
        Traditionsz: Aspects of Racial Elements with Influence on a
        Guianese Community.* vol. 1 Georgetown, Guyana: n.p.,
        1962.

        Essentially a book on music; however, the Cumfa ceremony of
        Congo origin, the East Indian Tadjah festival, and Christmas
        festivities described.

234. "Brazilian Bosso Nova Creators Charge Yankee Murder of Dance."
        Chicago Defender (Jan. 18, 1963): 9.

        Lenny Dale's bosso nova dance, based on the traditional
        samba, is well liked in Rio de Janeiro; the Yankee jazz musicians'
        interpretation of the dance music is not.

235. Bricklin, Mark. "Arthur Hall & Company: Afro-American
        Ensemble in Another Dance Triumph." *Philadelphia Tribune*
        (Jan. 21, 1967): 2nd section.

236. "Broadway's Wildest Ballroom." *Ebony* (Dec. 1953): 40-42.

Features the Palladium, which billed itself as "the home of the mambo."

237. Bronkhurst, H.V.P. *The Colony of British Guyana and Its Labouring Population: Containing a Short Account of the Colony, and Brief Descriptions of the Black Creole, Portuguese, East Indian, and Chinese Coolies.* London: T. Woolman, 1883.

Mentions obeah dances, balls, and tea-meetings (pp. 286-89).

238. "Brooklynite Has Starring Role in City Ballet." *New York Amsterdam News* (June 23, 1979): 42.

Profiles Debra Austin's career as a member of the New York City Ballet. Reviews her performance in Balanchine's "Stars and Stripes."

239. Brooks, Valerie. "Virginia Johnson Starring in N.Y." *New York Daily News* [Sunday's People] (June 16, 1985): 4-5.

Profiles the Dance Theatre of Harlem star who danced with the company since its inception.

240. Brower, Brock. "On Stage: Matt Turney." *Horizon* (Nov. 1962): 68.

241. Brown, Ardie. "Joan Meyers Brown: Critics and Audiences." *Dance Dialogue* 1, no. 2 (Summer 1979): 6-10.

Interviews Joan Meyers Brown of Philadanco on the issue: whether or not white critics can understand black dance.

242. Brown, Cecelia R. "The First National Congress of Blacks in Dance." *Dance Dimensions* 2, no. 1 (Fall 1973): [12]-[13].

Reports on the congress held at Indiana University, June 26-July 1, 1973, sponsored by the Modern Organization for Dance Evolvement and the Black Music Center of Indiana University.

243. ———. "The Afro-American Contribution to Dance in the United States, 1619-1965." *Negro Heritage* 14, no. 3 (1975): 63-71.

244. Brown, Elizabeth White and Allen Ericson Weatherford, II. "Dance Education—Its Nature, Scope and Sociological Implications in Negro Colleges and Universities in North Carolina." *Quarterly Review of Higher Education Among Negroes* (Apr. 1951): 65-80.

245. Brown, Esther. "Dancing for Integration: Report from Kentucky." *Dance Magazine* (July 1956): 56-57, 59.

Reports on a program danced by black students from Kentucky State College and white students from the University of Kentucky for the purpose of education for integration. The blacks danced African, West Indian, mambo, cha cha, etc. The author expounds on the idea that dance provides a common meeting ground by which people can understand each other better.

246. Brown, Eunice. "An Experiment in Negro Modern Dance." *Dance Observer* (Jan. 1946): 4-5.

Report on the work of a black modern dance group started under the auspices of the Modern Dance Center in Minneapolis in 1937. It addresses the question of whether or not black concert dance should exist and if training for black dancers should be different from that of whites.

247. Brown, Henry. "Many Dance Stars Owe Start to Hazel T. Davis." *Chicago Defender* (May 20, 1933): 11.

Relates the career of Hazel Thompson Davis, dance teacher of many Broadway stars.

248. Brown, John Mason. "Bill Robinson as a Really 'Hot Mikado.'" *New York Post* (Mar. 27, 1939).

249. ———. "Zunguru Danced at the Chanin Auditorium." *New York Post* (Apr. 9, 1940).

   Reviews the work by Asadata Dafora.

250. Brown, Sterling A. "The Negro on the Stage." In *The Negro in American Culture.* Carnegie-Myrdal Study: *The Negro in America,* 1940.

   Chapter 2, "Negroes in Song and Dance," gives a historical overview of the black on stage beginning with minstrelsy. Chapter 4, "Negro Musical Shows: New Style," discusses major contributions to the musical stage including "Shuffle Along," 1921.

251. Browning, Graeme. "Ailey Dance Theater: 'Dazzling Display.'" *The Tennessean* (Mar. 25, 1981).

252. Brozo, James. "Vereen's Cool Easy on Himself." *New York Daily News* (Aug. 17, 1980).

253. "Bubbles Bounces Back." *Ebony* (Jan. 1965): 49-54.

   John Bubbles makes a career comeback on tour with Anna Maria Alberghetti.

254. Buckle, Richard, ed. *Katherine Dunham, Her Dancers, Singers, Musicians.* Illus. by Roger Wood and other photographers. London: Ballet Publications, [1949].

   Consists chiefly of photos taken during Dunham's London season in Sept. 1948. Buckle gives an overview of her career and the scenarios of her works.

255. "Buddy Bradley; Nimble Ex-Harlemite Runs Most Successful Dance School in England with 500 Students." *Ebony* (July 1950): 61-64.

256. "Buddy Bradley Tours Europe." *Ebony* (Nov. 1954): 135-38.

257. Bunce, Alan. "Black Expo—'But Never Jam Today.'" *Christian Science Monitor* (Apr. 28, 1969).

Review of a performance of the Afro-American Folkloric Troupe at the Black Expo at City Center in New York, 1969.

258. Burridge, Sandra. "Limber of the Lambi." *News of Haiti* (Aug. 30, 1969).

Lavinia Williams discusses the benefits of dance as exercise.

259. Burroughs, Alison. "Notes on the Dance in the Negro Theatre." *Dance Herald* (Jan. 1938).

260. Burwell, Letitia. *A Girl's Life in Virginia before the War.* 2nd ed. New York: F.A. Stokes Company, 190?.

These reminiscences of plantation life in Va. have an account of dancing at the deathbed of a slave (p. 163) and a description of corn-shucking festivities (pp. 130, 131).

261. Butcher, Margaret (Just). *The Negro in American Culture; Based on Materials Left by Alain Locke.* New York: Knopf, 1956.

Investigates the impact of black creativity on American life. Chapter 3, "Early Folk Gifts: Music, Dance, Folklore" and Chapter 4, "Negro Music and Dance: Formal Recognition and Reconstruction," are helpful.

262. Butler, Albert and Josephine Butler. *Encyclopedia of Social Dance.* New York: Albert Butler Ballroom Dance Service, 1975.

Steps and origins of various social dances popular in the United States.

263. Cable, George Washington. "The Dance in Place Congo." *The Century* 31, no. 4 (Feb. 1886): 517-532.

Discusses the tribal background of and describes the slaves who would gather and dance in Congo Square, New Orleans.

264. Cabot, Morrison. "DanceAfrica Brings Barefoot Soul to BAM." *New York Amsterdam News* (Apr. 18, 1981).

Announces a three-day festival of African dance at the Brooklyn Academy of Music.

265. Cabral, Sergio. *As Escolas de Samba.* Rio de Janeiro: Editora Fontana, 1974.

Describes the samba schools of Brazil.

266. Cahill, Kathleen. "Dreamgirls (and Boys) Take B'way Dance Class." *News World* (Feb. 24, 1982).

Describes a dance class conducted by Michael Peters, choreographer of *Dreamgirls*.

267. "Cakewalk King: 81 Year Old Charles Johnson Still Dreams of New Comeback with Dance Step of Gay '90s." *Ebony* (Feb. 1953): 99-102.

Recounts the career of Charles E. Johnson and his wife, Dora Dean, the first to bring the cakewalk to Broadway in 1895. Includes a brief history of the cakewalk.

268. Calloway, Earl. "Scotty, 'Dancin' Tailor' Is Doing Fine." *Chicago Defender* (Feb. 28, 1984): 14.

Profiles a Chicago dancer and tailor who has danced with and sewn for famous dancers.

269. Cameron, John. "Voodoo Adds to the Magic of Bahia." *New York Sunday News* (Aug. 22, 1976).

Describes candomblé ceremonies witnessed in Bahia, Brazil.

270.   Campbell, Dick. "Eugene Von Grona and Black Dance History."
New York Amsterdam News (Dec. 12, 1981): 36.

Gives an overview of dance in New York at the time when Von
Grona introduced his American Negro Ballet at the Lafayette
Theatre.

271.   Campbell, E. Simms. "Swing Mr. Charlie!" *Esquire* (Feb.
1936): 100, 183.

Describes truckin' and the lindy hop as danced in Harlem.
Campbell, an artist, illustrates the article.

272.   Canessa, Francesco. "In Metrò Sognando l'Africa." *Roma* (Oct.
17, 1980): n.p.

Reviews the Chuck Davis Dance Company in Naples.

273.   Carámbula, Rubén. *Negro y Tambor*. Buenos Aires: Editorial
Folklorica Americana, 1952.

Describes candombe, pp. 177-92.

274.   Cardona, Carlos Mota. "A Gift from Dakar." *The Feet* (June
1973): 12, 31.

Reviews a performance of the National Dance Company of
Senegal.

275.   Carli, Fabrizio. "La Tradizione, il Ritmo, la Fantasia." *L'Ora*
[Palermo] (Oct. 20, 1980).

Reviews the Chuck Davis Dance Company performing in
Palermo, Italy.

276.   "Carmen De Lavallade." *Jet* (July 31, 1952): 34-35.

277.   "Carmen De Lavallade Teaches Dancing to Children as a Hobby."
Sepia Record (Aug. 1954): 20-21.

278. Carmichael, Mrs. A.C. *Domestic Manners and Social Conditions of the White, Coloured and Negro Population of the West Indies,* 2 vols. London: Whittaker, Treacher and Co., 1833.

Vol. 1 (pp. 292-97) describes slave dancing and slave life on St. Vincent and Trinidad. Vol. 2 (pp. 238-39) discusses dancing and the conduct of blacks in relation to the church.

279. Carneiro, Edison Da Souza. "Danças Folclóricas do Brasil." *Brazil Açucareiro* 70, no. 2 (Aug. 1967): 67-69.

280. ———. *Capoeira.* Rio de Janeiro: Campanha de Defesa do Folclore Brasileiro, 1971.

281. "Carolyn Adams: American Dance's Best-Kept Secret." *New York Amsterdam News* (Apr. 11, 1981): 29.

The life and career of Carolyn Adams, member of the Paul Taylor Dance Company for 16 years.

282. Carreño, Francisco. "La Influencia Negra en el Merengue Venezolano y la Música de San Javier." *Revista Venezolano de Folklore* [Caracas], 1, no. 2 (1947): 79-84.

Discusses the African rhythms in the Venezuelan merengue.

283. "Carriacou Dances." *Caribbean Quarterly* 3, no. 1 (1953-54): 31-34.

Photo of the big drum dance and nation dances.

284. Carroll, Noël. "Tap Is Black...." *Dance Magazine* (Jan. 1981): 93-97.

Reviews the tap-dancing festival "By Word of Foot" at the Village Gate, New York City, Oct. 13-18, 1980, and the film "No Maps on My Taps."

285. ———. "Review of Alvin Ailey American Dance Theater and Philadelphia Dance Company (Philadanco)." *Dance Magazine* (Mar. 1981): 38-44.

286. Carter, Elmer A. "He Smashed the Color Line: A Sketch of Billy Pierce." *Opportunity* (May 1930): 148-149.

Billy Pierce, dance teacher, ran a successful dance studio on Broadway that trained dancers and stars for the Broadway stage.

287. Carvalho-Neto, Paulo de. "La Comparsa Lubola del Carnival Montevideano." *Archivos Venezolanos de Folklore* 10-11, no. 7 (1961-62): 153-86.

Describes dramatic Montevideo carnival dances of African origin.

288. ———. *El Negro Uruguayo (Hasta la Abolición).* Quito, Ecuador: Editorial Universitaria, 1965.

Part 4 (pp. 293-328) discusses several dances including batuque, la chica, bámbula, and calenda.

289. ———. "El Carnaval de Montevideo: Folklore, Historia, Sociologia." In *Publicaciones de Seminario de Anthropolgia Americana, no. 9.* Seville: University of Seville, 1967.

Describes the carnival in Montevideo, which is of African origin, and compares it to the carnival at Rio de Janeiro.

290. ———. *Estudios Afros: Brasil-Paraguay-Uruguay-Ecuador.* Caracas: Instituto de Anthropologia E Historia. Facultad de Humanidades y Educacion, Universidad Central de Venezuela, 1971.

Describes *El Candombe,* an Afro-Uruguayan folkloric dance-drama (pp. 181-94).

291. Carybé, O. *Jogo da Capoeira; 24 Desenhos de Coleção Recôncavo n. 3.* Bahia, Brazil: Livraria Progresso Editora, 1955.

Drawings of musicians and participants in capoeira.

292. Caspary, Vera. "The Black, Black Bottom of the Swanee River." *The Dance* (Mar. 1927): 15-16.

Discusses the history and origin of the black bottom as a dance. The author states that it came from the black section of Atlanta, known as the Black Bottom, and that it developed as a stomp. It was supposedly changed from being a simple dance to a sensational one by those who performed it on stage in the North.

293. Cassidy, Frederic G. *Jamaica Talk.* London: Macmillan, 1961.

Studies Jamaican words and discusses Jamaican customs. Chapter 12, "John Canoe: Other Entertainments," describes the John Canoe and individual dances, such as the shay-shay, brukins, and yanga, common in Jamaica.

294. Castellanos, Henry C. *New Orleans as It Was.* New Orleans: L. Graham and Sons, 1895.

A chapter of this social history of New Orleans describes Congo Square dancing and the dances of voodoo.

295. "The Cat Lady of Philadelphia." *Ebony* (Dec. 1965): 76-84.

Princess Starletta De Paur, paraplegic ex-dancer, raises cats and turns her profits over to a charitable foundation for the purchase of wheelchairs, crutches, etc.

296. Cayou, Dolores Kirton. "The Origins of Modern Jazz Dance." *Black Scholar* 1, no. 8 (June 1970): 26-31.

Traces the origins of modern jazz dance to Africa, giving the characteristics of traditional African dance and tracing the development of dance in slavery, minstrel shows, vaudeville, etc. to the 1930s.

297. ———. *Modern Jazz Dance*. Palo Alto, Calif.: National Press Books, 1971.

The author sees jazz as the total expression of a group and related to their experience. Includes a brief history of the development of modern jazz dance from its roots in African culture. Lists the characteristics of traditional African dance and how dance developed in the United States, with references to social and stage dance. The major part of the book consists of technique exercises, rhythmic exercises, turns, walks, combinations, and class planning.

298. "Celebration and Challenge, Twenty Years of Jamaica's National Dance Theatre Company." *Caribe* 7, (nos. 1 & 2): 21-23.

Gives a history of the company and a biographical sketch of Rex M. Nettleford, its founder.

299. "Celebrities and 8 Miles of Crowds Pay Last Tribute to Bill Robinson." *New York Times* (Nov. 29, 1949).

300. "Cha Cha Cha Dance Craze Is Cuban Flavored Slow Drag." *Ebony* (Feb. 1956): 26-28.

301. Chase, Gilbert. *America's Music from the Pilgrims to the Present*. Revised 2nd ed. New York: McGraw-Hill, 1966.

Mentions various dances in the chapters on spirituals, blues, and jazz. Describes a shout (pp. 256-57) and dancing in Place Congo (pp. 305-08).

302. Checker, Chubby and Geoffrey Holder. "To Twist or Not to Twist." *Ebony* (Feb. 1962): 106-10.

303. Chenzira, Ayoka. "Syvilla Fort: Spirit on the Dance Floor." *Dance Book Forum* 1 (1981): 5-6.

304. Chequer, John D. "Arias and Encores: Negro Ballet Presents Distinctive Program in Wood Auditorium—Four Compositions

Offer Wide Variety of Dance Forms, Small Audience Pleased." *Daily Argus* [Mount Vernon, N.Y.] (Feb. 26, 1938).

The American Negro Ballet.

305. "Chicken; Borrowed from a Barnyard, Novel Dance Sweeps Detroit." *Ebony* (Feb. 1955): 81-83.

306. "Chilton and Thomas Give Harlem a Taste of Dance." *The Chicago Defender* (Feb. 25, 1933).

The career and lives of Carol Chilton and Maceo Thomas.

307. "China Doll." *Our World* (Dec. 1952): 65-66.

On Liz Dickerson, a dancer at Small's Paradise in Harlem.

308. "Choreographers Confer." *New York Amsterdam News* (Nov. 25, 1978): D-5.

The First International Choreographers' Conference was held in New York City and had delegations from 25 countries. This conference was notable in that no black-American choreographers were represented.

309. "Chorus Girl's Goodbye." *Ebony* (Nov. 1955): 72-76.

Freddie Cole ends 21-year career at the Club DeLisa, Chicago.

310. Christensen, Mrs. Abigail M. Holmes. "Spirituals and 'Shouts' of Southern Negroes." *Journal of American Folklore* 7 (1894): 154-55.

Describes a ring shout in a Southern praise house. Mentions that the ring shout is dying out with the changing times.

311. "Chubby Checker and the Twist." *Sepia* (Jan. 1962): 78-82.

312. "Chuck Davis Dancers Tour Europe." *Bronx Arts* [Bronx Council on the Arts Newsletter] (Nov.1980).

313. Chujoy, Anatole. "Ballet Theatre Arrives." *Dance* [East Stroudsburg, Pa.] (Feb. 1940): 32-39.

Reviews the debut of Ballet Theatre's first season, in which a black cast danced Agnes DeMille's "Black Ritual."

314. Clarity, James F. "Moscow Audience Hails Ailey Dancers." *New York Times* (Oct. 22, 1970).

315. Clark, VeVe A. "Katherine Dunham's 'Tropical Revue.'" *Caribe* 7 (nos. I & II): 15. Reprinted from *Black American Literature Forum* 16, no. 4 (Winter 1982).

316. Clark, Wilhelmina O. "Physical Education through Dance." *Negro Educational Review* (Apr. 1950): 100-02.

317. Clarke, Mary. "Black New World." *Dancing Times* (Oct. 1967): 15.

Reviews Donald McKayle's work performed at the Strand Theatre, London, Aug. 30, 1967.

318. Clinton, Audrey. "Hub's Opening Night." *Newsday* (July 24, 1982).

Reviews Ben Vereen at the Hub Entertainment Center, Hempstead, Long Island.

319. Cluzel, Magdeleine. *Glimpses of the Theatre and Dance.* New York: Kamin Publishers, 1953. Translation of *Panorama de la Danse en Mil Neuf Cent Cinquante-Deux.* [Paris]: M. Daranthière, 1952.

Discusses André Quellier's drawings of Katherine Dunham. Also gives a brief biography of Dunham and a description of her works.

320. Cole, Carriebel B. *Dances Worth While*.... Washington, D.C.: Murray Bros. Press, 1918.

Gives the steps of two black dances with music.

321. Cohn, Ellen. "Alvin Ailey Arsonist." *New York Times Magazine* (Apr. 29, 1973).

Profiles Alvin Ailey.

322. Coleman, J. Winston. *Slave Times in Kentucky*. Chapel Hill, N.C.: University of North Carolina Press, 1940.

The chapter on slave life includes material on songs, dances, and Christmas celebrations.

323. Coley, Cornell. "Capoeira." *Caribe* 7 (no. I & II): 41-42.

324. Collins, Lisa. "Coloring Dance Black and White." *Sepia* (May 1979): 31-38.

Surveys the current American dance scene and how blacks in it fare against long-standing ideas about what kind of dance they should perform.

325. "Colored Artists Play Big Part in Workers' Dance in New York." *Washington Tribune* (Oct. 2, 1933).

The report of a forum sponsored by the Workers' Dance League at the Harlem YWCA addressing the question "What shall the Negro dance about?" Hemsley Winfield, the early black concert dancer, participated.

326. "Colourful Ballet Negro Dancers Provide Brilliant Spectacle." *The Scotsman* (Sept. 24, 1957).

Reviews the New York Negro Ballet performing in Edinburgh.

327.   Como, William. "More on Calypso." *Dance Magazine* (Mar. 1957): 54-55.

How to dance ballroom calypso.

328.   "Composer Here for Showing of 'La Guiablesse.'" *Chicago Defender* (Dec. 8, 1934).

Katherine Dunham dances the lead in William Grant Still's work.

329.   Comvalius, Theod A.C. "Oud-Surnaamsche Rhythmische Dansen in Dienst van de Lichamelijke Opvoeding." (Old Surnamese Rhythmic Dances in the Service of Physical Education). *De West-Indische Gids* 27 (1946): 97-103.

330.   *A Concise Account of All the British Colonies in North America.* Dublin: C. Jenkins, 1776.

Describes the jig-dancing among white people in Va., a dance originally borrowed from blacks (pp. 212-13). The same passages are reprinted in James Franklin's *The Philosophical and Political History of the Thirteen United States of America* (London: 1784, p. 91).

331.   Conzemius, Eduard. "Ethnographical Notes on the Black Carib." *American Anthropologist* 30 (Apr.-June 1928): 183-205.

Gives the origins of the Black Carib of Honduras and describes their gujai dancing, said to have been introduced by the Haitians. Also describes the wanaragua (John Canoe) and other dances.

332.   Cook, Will Marion. "Clorindy, the Origin of the Cakewalk." *Theatre Arts* 31 (Sept. 1947): 61-65.

Recounts his struggle to get the first all-black show on Broadway in 1898.

333.   "Co-op; Youthful Chicago Trio Makes Highly Popular Stage Act Out of Modern Dance Routines." *Ebony* (Feb. 1951): 43-44.

334. Cooper, H.E. "Minstrel Days." *The Dance* (Nov. 1926): 22-23, 54-55.

Gives the theatrical development of minstrel shows as entertainment ("only original American form of entertainment"). Within the minstrel show various dances were developed: the jig, clog dancing, and soft shoe shuffle. The author suggests that the minstrel show gave "nourishment to every present form of musical presentation."

335. Coopersmith, Jacob Maurice. *Music and Musicians of the Dominican Republic.* Washington, D.C.: Pan American Union. Division of Music and Visual Department of Cultural Arts Affairs, 1949.

This is mainly a general work on the music of the Dominican Republic. There is some attention to dance (pp. 53-60).

336. "Cotton Club Boys; Members of Famed Dancing Group Hold First Reunion." *Ebony* (Jan. 1954): 116-121.

The Cotton Club Boys pioneered precision chorus dancing.

337. Courlander, Harold. *The Drum and the Hoe: Life and Lore of the Haitian People.* Berkeley, Calif.: University of California Press, 1960.

Presents a broad view of certain aspects of Haitian culture. Chapter 11, "Dancing and Dance Drama," discusses the role of dance in Haitian life. Describes the dances, postures, and dance characteristics of certain cults. Also gives a list of dances associated with each of the following rituals: voodoo, congo and petro, juba, rara, carnival dances, and secular dances.

338. ———. *Negro Folk Music, U.S.A.* New York: Columbia University Press, 1963.

Chapter 10, "Dances: Calindas, Buzzard Lopes, and Reels," discusses "dances that were an integral part of Negro culture whether derived from African or European sources."

339. Covarrubias, Miguel. *Negro Drawings*. New York: A.A. Knopf, 1927.

Drawings by a Mexican artist of black activities, including dance and music.

340. Cox, Leonore. "On a Few Aspects of Negro Dancing." In *Proceedings of the National Dance Congress and Festival, 1st, 1936*, 52-55.

Contends that black dancers need not be bound to jazz dance or primitive dance. Discusses various dancers and groups who were pioneering in modern and concert dancing, such as Hemsley Winfield, Asadata Dafora, and the Hampton Institute dancers. Says that black dancers should choose themes significant to blacks.

341. ———. "Merrily We Dance." *Dance Herald* (Mar. 1938): 3.

Summarizes the black influence and contributions to jazz and popular dance.

342. Craig, Alberta Ratliffe. "Old Wentworth Sketches." *North Carolina Historical Review* 11, no. 3 (July 1934): 185-204.

These reminiscences of a childhood in Wentworth, N.C. describe blacks at a corn-shucking party and dancing the "holy dance."

343. Craig-Raymond, Peter. "A Cliché Comes to Life." *Ballet Today* 6, no. 11 (Dec. 1953): 5.

Reviews Claude Marchant and "Tropical Rhythms."

344. ———. "Braziliana." *Ballet Today* 6, no. 11 (Dec. 1953): 4.

Reviews Braziliana Teatro Folclorico Brasileiro in London.

345. "Crazy, Man, Crazy; On New York's Great White Way the Palladium is Pandemonium when Mambo Fans Take Charge." *Our World* (Dec. 1953): 10-11.

346. Creecy, James R. *Scenes in the South.* Washington, D.C.: Thomas McGill, Printer, 1860.

 Describes manners, customs, and plantation life in the South with a description of dancing in Congo Square, New Orleans (pp. 12-23).

347. Crittenden, John. "Ailey Troupe Dances into TV." *Sunday Record* [Bergen County, N.J.] (May 5, 1974): B-25.

 Interview with Alvin Ailey prior to a scheduled television appearance.

348. "Crowd Cheers John Bubbles, Judy Garland." *Jet* (Aug. 24, 1967): 60-61.

 At the Palace Theatre in New York City.

349. Crowder, Tinsley. "Diana Ramos Solo Recital Program. The Cubiculo, June 28, 1972." *Dance Magazine* (Sept. 1972): 24.

350. Crowley, Daniel J. "Festivals of the Calendar in St. Lucia." *Caribbean Quarterly* 4, no. 2 (1955): 99-121.

 Describes feast days, holidays, carnivals, and their dances for one year.

351. ———. "Calypso: Trinidad Carnival Songs and Dances." *Dance Notation Record* 9, no. 2 (1958): 3-7.

352. Crowther, Bosley. "From the 'Turkey Trot' to the 'Big Apple.'" *New York Times Magazine* (Nov. 7, 1937).

 Describes the dance the big apple and discusses its place in the tradition of dances like the turkey trot and the tango.

353. "Cuban Dancers Make Like a Boat." *PM* (Dec. 26, 1946).

Dancers Machito and Estella dance El Botecito in this photographic essay.

354. "Cuba's Princess Orelia Shows Sexy 'Love Dance.'" *Jet* (May 28, 1953): 60.

Does a version of nañigo.

355. "Cumfa—A Voodoo Twin? *Daily Chronicle* [Georgetown, Guyana] (June 14, 1973).

Lavinia Williams gives her impressions of Cumfa and tells of her work researching Haitian folklore.

356. Cunningham, Katherine S. "The Dance at St. Paul's School." *Dance Magazine* (June 1970): 24-25.

Billy Wilson, dancer-choreographer, teaches dance classes at the exclusive boys' prep school. Reveals his approach to teaching.

357. Dana, M. "Voodoo." *Metropolitan Magazine* [New York] 28 (1908): 529-35.

358. "Dance." *IDS* [Indiana University] (Apr. 27, 1977).

Profiles the Afro-American Dance Company of Indiana University.

359. Dance Caravan. *Progress and Development of Dancemobile, 1967-68.* [New York: n.p., 1969].

A report submitted to the New York State Council on the Arts describes the history, organization and policy, internal structure, problems, recommendations, and artists who performed in the 1967-68 seasons of the Dancemobile.

360. "Dance in Brazil; an Overall Look." *Dance Herald* 1 (3): 2-4.

361. Dance Masters of America. *Jazz Syllabus*. N.p: Dance Masters of America, Inc., 1976.

362. "Dance of Love." *Hue* (June 30, 1954): 10-13.

Carmen De Lavallade and James Truitt perform a Panamanian mating cermony in Los Angeles.

363. "Dance of the Fire Gods." *Sepia* (May 1962): 52-54.

Dance team Prince Donell and Orlena perform this ritual Balinese dance as part of their act. Gives details of their careers.

364. "Dance School." *Ebony* (Apr. 1954): 56-59.

Profiles Jimmy Payne, an experienced Chicago dancer who teaches entertainers routines for their acts.

365. "Dance Star Bears Pain to Perform." *News and Observer* [Raleigh, N.C.] (Nov. 27, 1983).

Mel Tomlinson of the New York City Ballet.

366. "Dance Version of 'Porgy.'" *Ebony* (Sept. 1953): 99-101.

A young New York interracial ballet group produces a dance version of *Porgy and Bess*.

367. "Dance Virtuoso." *Ebony* (Feb. 1957): 32, 35-37.

Eunice Cain of Minneapolis-St. Paul is a dancer and dance teacher.

368. "Dancer Bill Bailey Jailed in N.Y.C. as Dope Addict." *Jet* (Jan. 26, 1956): 58

369. "Dancer Charles Johnson Dies, Strutted Cakewalk in the '90's." *New York Post* (Dec. 30, 1959).

370. "Dancer Hits the Ceiling." *Jet* (Dec. 2, 1954): 34-35.

Shawneequa Baker dances with Jean-Léon Destiné's Haitian dancers.

371. "Dancer Takes Top Met Spot." *New York Age* (Oct. 6, 1951): 8.

Announces that Janet Collins is one of the *première danseuses* at the Metropolitan Opera.

372. "Dancers Eye Prison Plan: Instruments Off to Tokyo." *Philadelphia Inquirer* (Dec. 26, 1971).

Describes Arthur Hall's Afro-American Dance Ensemble.

373. "Dancers Go Dramatic." *Ebony* (Sept. 1969): 38-42.

Lola Falana and Fayard Nicholas perform their first dramatic roles in a movie.

374. "Dancing at the Pillow." *Our World* (Dec. 1954): 8-10.

The Negro Dance Theater, an all-male group founded by Aubrey Hitchins, debuts at Jacob's Pillow Dance Festival in Lee, Mass.

375. "The Dancing Holders." *Ebony* (Feb. 1958): 117-22.

Profiles Carmen De Lavallade and Geoffrey Holder. Photographic series of the Holders dancing Trinidad's Bélé.

376. Dantas, Beatriz G. "Dança de São Gonçalo." *Cadernos de Folclore, n.s.* 9 (1976).

377. "Darwin and the Mambo." *Time* (Sept. 6, 1954): 34.

378. Dauer, Alfons M. "Book Review" Gunther, Helmut. *Grudehanomene un Grundbegriffe des Afrikanischen und Afro-Amerikanischen Tanzes.* Graz: Universal Edition, 1969." *Ethnomusicology* 19, no. 2 (May 1975): 308.

379. Davenport, Frederick Morgan. *Primitive Traits in Religious Revivals*. New York: Macmillan, 1905.

Presents a sociological interpretation of religious revivals. Chapter 5, "The Religion of the American Negro," describes the flower dance, the roper dance, and other dances that take place in religious worship.

380. David, Clement. "Haiti in Brilliant Farewell Show." *Daily Chronicle* [Georgetown, Guyana] (Sept. 9, 1972).

Lavinia Williams's Ballet d'Haiti performs at Carifesta, the Caribbean arts festival.

381. Davin, Tom. "Conversations with James P. Johnson." *Jazz Review* 2, no. 5 (1959): 14-17; 2, no. 6 (1959): 10-13; 2, no. 7 (1959): 13-15; 2, no. 8 (1959): 26-27.

James P. Johnson remembers music and musicians in New York City in the early 1900s. Comments on style of dress and on various popular dances like the cakewalk and charleston.

382. Davis, Betty. "Expression '83." *Attitude* 2, no. 6 (Nov. 1983): 26.

Reviews the annual festival sponsored by the Caribbean Cultural Center. Groups performing: Dominican Street Dancers, Brazilian Troupe, and Marie Brooks Dance Theater.

383. Davis, Curt. "Community Helps Harlem Dance Theatre to Its Feet." *New York Post* (Oct. 4, 1983).

The corporate sector and private citizens help the Dance Theatre of Harlem after its studios were vandalized.

384. Davis, Henry C. "Negro Folk-lore in South Carolina." *Journal of American Folklore* 27 (1914): 241-54.

Describes plantation dances.

385. Day, Charles William. *Five Years' Residence in the West Indies.*
2 vols. London: Colburn, 1852.

Describes the following West Indian customs and dances:
jumbee dance (vol. 1, pp. 85-86), Negro ladies ball (vol. 1, pp.
294-95), the Trinidad carnival (vol. 1, pp. 313-16), and Christmas
in Barbuda (vol. 2, p. 297).

386. "Dazzling New Star of Dance Drama." *Ebony* (July 1958): 28.

Profiles Matt Turney, star of the Martha Graham Company.

387. "Death Takes Billy Pierce, 'Dance King.'" *Philadelphia Tribune*
(Apr. 13, 1933).

Teacher of many Broadway stars. Claims Pierce created the
charleston, black bottom, and sugar foot stomp.

388. Dehn, Mura. "Night Life in Georgia." *Jazz Monthly* 6, no. 9
(1960): 11-12.

Brief account of a visit to Georgia to see black dancing in a
night club.

389. ———. "A Propos d'un Film sur la Danse des Noirs Americains."
Jazz Hot 26, no. 158 (Oct. 1960): 16-19.

Recounts the making of a film on black-American dancing with
James Berry.

390. ———. "'Be for Real,' An Interview with James Berry." *Dance
Magazine* 35 (Sept. 1961): 48-49, 70, 71, 73.

391. DeJon, Lythe Orme. "The Gombeys of Bermuda." *Dance
Magazine* (May 1956): 32-34, 54-55.

Gives the history of gombey dancing; describes gombey
dancing during Christmas.

392. Delaunay-Belleville, André. *Choses et Gens de la Martinque.* Paris: Nouvelles Editions Debresse, 1963.

Chapter 10, "Moeurs, Coutumes et Folklore Martiniquais," describes the carnival and its dances, including the biguine, bélé or bellir, bombée, and serrée.

393. Denby, Edwin. "In Brightest Africa." *New York Herald Tribune* (Dec. 14, 1943).

Reviews the African Dance Festival at Carnegie Hall, Dec. 13, 1943, directed by Asadata Dafora.

394. Deren, Maya. *Divine Horsemen; the Living Gods of Haiti.* London: Thames and Hudson, 1953.

Delineates the metaphysical principles underlying the practices of voodoo. Dances are described within the context of the religion.

395. "Destiné Airs Dance." *Afro-American* (June 4, 1949): 6.

Destiné performed on a CBS television program. Gives a brief resumé of his career.

396. Destiné Has Close Brush with Death." *New York Amsterdam News* (Jan. 17, 1959).

397. Devoe, Thomas F. *The Market Book, Containing a Historical Account of the Public Markets in the Cities of New York, Boston, Philadelphia and Brooklyn.* New York: Printed for the author, 1862.

Gives accounts of festivities, dancing, and slave street gangs in New York City's public markets in the 1700s (pp. 264-65, 344, 345). Describes dancing in the Bear Market (p. 322) and in the Catherine Market (p. 344) where "the first introduction in this city of public 'Negro dancing'" took place. Gives the names of those slaves with good reputations as dancers.

398.   Dexter, Charles E. "Negro Dance Unit Performs an African Dance Drama." *Daily Worker* (Dec. 10, 1936).

Reviews Asadata Dafora's company.

399.   "Dickie Wells Makes Return to Headlines." *New York Amsterdam News* (Aug. 30, 1947).

Former vaudeville dancer associated with the trio Mordecai, Wells and Taylor and many elaborate revues plans a return to the stage.

400.   Dickinson, Katharine. "Magic of the Meringue." *Dance Magazine* 30 (Oct. 1956): 89-91.

Describes the Haitian version of the merengue, perceiving no difference between the Haitian and the Dominican versions. Offers some combinations discovered on a visit to Haiti.

401.   Dickson, William. *Letters on Slavery.* London: Printed and sold by J. Phillips, 1789.

Describes dancing and merrymaking on Sundays and holidays in Barbados (pp. 93-94).

402.   Diegues Junior, Manuel. "Danças Negras No Nordeste." In *Congresso Afro-brasileiro,* 2nd ed., Bahia, 1937.

403.   Diggs, Irene. "Singing and Dancing in Afro-Cuba." *The Crisis* (Dec. 1951).

Examines the social aspects of Afro-Cuban dancing in this review of *Los Bailes y el Teatro de los Negros in el Folklore de Cuba* by Fernando Ortiz.

404.   Dimitry, E.L. "Like Witch Stories?" *Chicago Defender* (June 16, 1934).

Reviews Asadata Dafora's "Kykunkor" as it opens on Broadway.

405. Dirks, Robert. "Slaves' Holiday." *Natural History* 84, no. 10 (Dec. 1975): 82-84, 87-88, 90, 95.

Discusses John Canoe and the set-girls celebrations in this detailed account of the slaves' Christmas in Jamaica.

406. Dixon, Frankye A. "New World Dancers Interpret Johnson Poem." *New York Amsterdam News* (Feb. 20, 1929).

Reviews a performance by the New World Dancers interpreting a poem, "Go Down Death," by James Weldon Johnson.

407. Dixon-Stowell, Brenda. "Between Two Eras: 'Norton and Margot' in the Afro-American Entertainment World." *Dance Research Journal* 15, no. 2 (Spring 1983): 1-20.

Gives the career of Margot Webb and Harold Norton, one of the few black-American ballroom dance teams in the history of dance. States that "their career was emblematic of the frustrations, paradoxes and double standards which existed for Afro-American artists in the United States."

408. Dmitri. "Characteristics of Brazilian Dance." *Dance Notation Record* 9, no. 2 (1958): 9-11.

Includes the notation of the steps of the marchinha and the frêvo, danced in carnival.

409. "Do You Remember U.S. Thompson?" *Negro Digest* (June 1951): 76-77.

Profiles the dancer who was the world's leading exponent of acrobatic dance and the husband of Florence Mills.

410. Dodge, Roger Pryor. "Jazz Dance/Mambo Dance." *Jazz Review* 2, no. 10 (1959): 59-63; 3, no. 1 (1960): 39-41.

The two articles discuss the dance and musical style of mambo and jazz dance. Also discusses the presentation of jazz dance by Whitey, Mura Dehn, and Marshall Stearns.

411. "Donald McKayle—Dancer." *Crisis* 60, no. 4 (Apr. 1953): 212-
13.

412. "Donald McKayle Premières New Dance Works at Brooklyn
Academy Festival." *New York Age* (Mar. 6, 1950).

Reviews the première of "The Street," "Prelude to Action,"
"Nocturne."

413. "Donald McKayle Stages Black Musical." *Chicago Defender*
(Dec. 6, 1979): 26.

Profiles the career of the choreographer on the occasion of the
staging of his musical "Evolution of the Blues."

414. "Dora Dean of Johnson and Dean Team Dead." *New York
Amsterdam News* (Dec. 17, 1949): 26.

Obituary of a partner of the famous cakewalk team.

415. Dorsey, Bobby. "Mary Bruce, Director of the Star Buds." *New
York Age* (Aug. 6, 1949): 20.

Mary Bruce also runs a well-known Harlem dancing school.

416. Doryk, Elinor. *Study of Historical and Present Day Dance in the
American Virgin Islands.* New York, 1951.

The material for this thesis, done for New York University
School of Education, was collected through interviews, personal
writings, personal observation, and newspaper articles. Relates the
history of island dancing. Discusses the history of the islands, the
place of dance in Africa and the New World, and basic African
rhythms in song and dance. Describes the dances currently done:
the quadrille, bamboula, masquerades, curacao, and mackshun.

417. Dowlin, John. "Rod Rodgers Dance Company: the Cubiculo
Theatre, Feb. 10, 17, 1969." *Dance Magazine* (Apr. 1969):
76-77.

418. Drutman, Irving. "Anthropology Plus Jazz." *Negro Digest* 2 (Dec. 1943): 47-48.

Katherine Dunham's dancing.

419. Dudley, Linda. "Ben Vereen: He's Branching Out All Over." *News World* (Jan. 17, 1980).

420. Duke, Jerry. "Clogging in the Appalachian Mountains." *Let's Dance* (Apr. 1974): 12-15.

According to the author's research, Appalachian clog dancing is an old form of English and/or Irish country dance influenced by black shuffle chugs and knee lifts.

421. The Duke of Iron. "Calypso!" *Argosy* (Sept. 1957): 42.

Consists of a Calypso song and photographs of limbo dancers in Trinidad.

422. Duncan, Kathy. "Solomons." *The Soho Weekly News* (June 20, 1974).

Reviews Gus Solomons, Jr.

423. "Dunham Dance Graduates." *Ebony* (June 1953): 48-53.

Reveals what happened to former Dunham dancers Eartha Kitt, Claude Marchant, Lavinia Williams, Carmencita Romero, Syvilla Fort, Janet Collins, and Talley Beatty.

424. "Dunham Dancers on Stage." *New York Post* (Oct. 19, 1940).

Summarizes Katherine Dunham's career and announces her forthcoming appearance in *Cabin in the Sky*.

425. Dunham, Katherine. "The Future of the Negro in Dance." *Dance Herald* (Mar. 1938): 5.

426. —— [Kaye Dunn, pseud.]. "La Boule Blanche." *Esquire* 12 (Sept. 1939): 92-93, 158.

Observes and describes beguine dancing in a popular dance hall in Martinique.

427. ——. [Kaye Dunn, pseud.]. "L'Ag'Ya of Martinique." *Esquire Magazine* 12 (Nov. 12, 1939): 84-85, 126.

428. ——. "The Negro Dances." In *The Negro Caravan* edited by Sterling A. Brown, Arthur P. Davis, and Ulysses Lee, 991-1000. New York: Dryden, 1941.

Gives an overview of black-American dancing.

429. ——. "Thesis Turned Broadway." *California Arts and Architecture* (Aug. 1941): 19, 37.

Discusses how form and function relate to modern theater by bringing to bear general knowledge of cultural patterns to theatrical productions.

430. ——. "Form and Function in Primitive Dance." *Educational Dance* (Oct. 1941): 2-4.

Discusses interrelationship of form and function, particularly in the dances of Haiti. Describes petro-magi of the Petro cult, yonvalou and Zepaules of the Rada cult and the congo paillette.

431. ——. *Journey to Accompong.* New York: Henry Holt, 1946.

Recounts her field trip to Accompong, Jamaica, to study the Maroons and their dances. Tells of her relationship with the Maroons, first seeing only their set dances and then, at the end of her stay, finally viewing some Myal dances and Kormantee war dances.

432. ——. "Ethnic Dancing." *Dance Magazine* 20 (Sept. 1946): 22, 34-35.

Reminiscences about Dunham's field trip to the West Indies and describes a funeral dance witnessed on the outskirts of Congo Village in Trinidad.

433.   ———. "The Dances of Haiti." *Acta Anthropologica* [Mexico] 2, no. 4 (1947): 1-60.

Katherine Dunham's study of Haitian sacred and secular dance covers the country, voodoo ritual and dances, the organization of dance groups, and their function and form.

434.   ———. *A Touch of Innocence.* New York: Harcourt, Brace and Company, 1959.

Account of the first 18 years of Dunham's life in Ill.

435.   ———. *Island Possessed.* Garden City, N.Y.: Doubleday, 1969.

In her memoirs of her time in Haiti 30 years before, Dunham describes the rites of voodoo, her initiation into the cult, the dances, and her feelings about Haitian dance and culture.

436.   Dunn, Beverly. "'Roots' Inspires Multi-Media Show." *IDS* [Indiana University] (Feb. 25, 1977).

Reviews the Afro-American Dance Company, Indiana University.

437.   Dunning, Jennifer. "Louis Johnson: 'I Love Dance—Any Kind of Dance.'" *New York Times* (Sept. 28, 1975).

438.   ———. "Dixie to Broadway, by Way of the Met." *New York Times* (Feb. 11, 1977).

Discusses the exhibit "Dixie to Broadway: An Exhibition of Black Americans on Stage, 1800-1939" shown at the Metropolitan Museum of Art during Black History Month, Feb. 1977.

439. ———. "What Johnson Dancers Do." *New York Times* (Apr. 6, 1977).

Profiles Raymond Johnson and his Raymond Johnson Dance Company prior to his Manhattan debut.

440. ———. "Dudley Williams—'You Can Only Go by Feeling.'" *New York Times Magazine* (May 7, 1978).

441. ———. "The Philadelphia Dance Company in a Debut at Clark Center Series." *New York Times* (July 30, 1978).

Reviews Philadanco's New York debut.

442. ———. "Dances by Faison, Lamb and Butler at the Ailey." *New York Times* (Dec. 2, 1978).

443. ———. "Dance: Ailey Company." *New York Times* (May 11, 1980).

Reviews the third of four programs at the City Center, New York City. The works performed: "District Storyville" (McKayle), "Night Creatures" (Ailey), "Love Songs" (Ailey), and "Fire Sermon" (Gene Hill Sagan).

444. ———. "The Exuberant Humor of Marilyn Banks." *New York Times* (Dec. 12, 1980): C12.

Interviews the Alvin Ailey dancer known for her comic dancing.

445. ———. "Dance Theatre of Harlem Opens Season Tomorrow." *New York Times* (Jan. 2, 1981).

Overview of the company's repertory and progress. Interview with Arthur Mitchell.

446. ———. "Harlem Dancers to Revive Scheherazade." *New York Times* (Jan. 4, 1981).

An article on the reasons for and the method of reviving Fokine's "Scheherazade."

447.   ———. "A Matched Pair, but Individuals." *New York Times* (Mar. 27, 1981).

Profiles the careers of Gregg Burge and Hinton Battle, the show-stopping dancers of "Sophisticated Ladies."

448.   ———. "Festival Salutes Black Classics of Dance." *New York Times* (Sept. 18, 1981): C5.

The Negro Ensemble Company's "A Salute to Black Classics of Dance and Music" was performed Sept. 17, 18, 19, 25, and 26, 1981 in New York City. Discusses briefly the careers and works of choreographers Andy Torres, John Parks, Eleo Pomare, and Shawneequa Baker-Scott.

449.   ———. "The Bucket Theater." *New York Times* (Feb. 11, 1982).

Reviews the Bottom of the Bucket. . .But Dance Theater, performing at the Theater of Riverside Church.

450.   ———. "A Tap Extravaganza in Brooklyn." *New York Times* (Feb. 19, 1982).

451.   ———. "Dance: Black Festival in Brooklyn." *New York Times* (Apr. 23, 1983).

Reviews the first six performances at the Brooklyn Academy of Music's Dance Black America. The works of Asadata Dafora, Talley Beatty, and Eleo Pomare were performed.

452.   ———. "Donors Warming to Harlem Troupe." *New York Times* (Aug. 16, 1983).

Dance Theatre of Harlem reports great success in fund-raising requirements.

453. "Dyane Harvey." *On Stage* (Mar. 1981).

   Interview.

454. "Dyerettes Train Successors; Pros Adopt Young Chorus Line."
   Ebony (Apr. 1961): 35-36.

455. Dzhermolinska, Helen. "The Merengue Becomes La Dominicana."
   Dance Magazine 21 (Sept. 1947): 27-47.

   Describes the ballroom dance La Dominicana, an adaptation of
   the merengue, and how it became the rage.

456. Edmiston, Dorothy. "A Texas Ballet." *Texas Monthly* 4 (Nov.
   1929): 458-64.

   Discusses Theodore Kosloff's plans for an African ballet.
   Outlines Kosloff's life and career and reasons for creating a ballet
   on that particular theme.

457. "87 Singers, 16 New, on Roster at 'Met.'" *New York Times*
   (Oct. 3, 1951).

   Mentions that Janet Collins was hired as *première danseuse*.

458. Elder, Jacob D. "Traditional Dance in the Trinidad Community.
   The Changing Attitude of the Middle Class to the Traditional
   Dance of Trinidad." *Extra-Mural Reporter* [Jamaica] 4 (1957):
   26-28.

459. Elías Ortiz, Sergio. "Informe Sobre el Festival Folclórico de
   Ibaqué." *Revista Colombiana de Folclor* [Bogota] 2, no. 4
   (Segunda Epoca 1960): 157-69.

   Describes a popular folk festival in Ibaqué, where the music is
   a mixture of African and Indian and the dances portray traditional
   regional myths and legends.

460. Elliot, Ann. "Real, Real Calypso: How It Is Sung and Danced in Trinidad." Parts 1 and 2. *Dance Magazine* (July, Oct. 1957): 30-[33], 90-93; 36-37, 72-75.

Author remembers growing up in Trinidad and relates the customs of carnival and calypso. Describes calypso dance.

461. Elliot, Debbie. "Afro-American Group at Jacob's Pillow." *Boston After Dark* (Aug. 31, 1971): 13.

Profiles Billy Wilson, choreographer, with his company, the Dance Company of the National Center of Afro-American Artists.

462. Ellmerich, Luis. *Historia da dança*. 3rd ed. São Paulo: Ricordi, 1969.

This general history of dance also covers origins and descriptions of black dances in Brazil.

463. Emery, Lynne Fauley. *Black Dance in the United States from 1619 to 1970*. Palo Alto, Calif.: National Press Books, 1972.

Gives the history of black dance from its African origins to 1970. Covers all forms of dance.

464. ———. "Black Dance and American Musical Theater to 1930." Paper presented to the Musical Theatre in America Conference, Apr. 4, 1981.

Gives brief history of blacks in the musical theater from minstrelsy on and mentions major black musicals and their contributions.

465. ———. "Review of *Jazz Dance* " by Marshall and Jean Stearns. *Dance Research, Journal of CORD* 13, no. 2 (Spring 1981): 33-34.

466. Engelbrecht, Barbara. "Swinging at the Savoy." *Dance Research Journal* 15, no. 2 (Spring 1983): 3-10.

Profiles the Savoy Ballroom, with a description of the lindy hop and its evolution.

467. "Entertaining You." *Glamour Magazine* (July 1958): 17-18.

Marshall Stearns discourses on rock and roll dances and relates them to old jazz dances.

468. Epstein, Dena J. "African Music in British and French America." *Musical Quarterly* (Jan. 1973): 61-91.

Describes slave dancing in the colonies while attempting to determine what kind of music the Africans brought to the colonies and how long it lasted.

469. ———. *Sinful Tunes and Spirituals: Black Folk Music to the Civil War.* Urbana, Ill.: University of Illinois Press, 1977.

This history of black folk music has many references to early dancing in America. The calinda is discussed on pp. 30-38; funerals and Pinkster celebrations (pp. 63-66); shouts and funerals (pp. 232-37); jigs (pp. 120-24); and Chapter 8, "Accultured Dancing and Associated Instruments," discusses patting juba.

470. Erenberg, Lewis A. "Everybody's Doin' It: The Pre-World War I Dance Craze, the Castles and the Modern Amercan Girl." *Feminist Studies* 3, nos. 1 & 2 (1975): 155-70.

Discusses how the dance craze began, how dancing was made public, how steps were borrowed from blacks, and how black music and dance were accepted.

471. Espinet, Charles. "Masquerade—Origins and Development of Trinidad's Carnival." *Canada-West Indies Magazine* 43, no. 13 (1953): 22-23, 25.

472. Esterow, Milton. "Chubby Checker Twists Upward." *New York Times* (Mar. 27, 1962).

473. Estrada, Ric. "3 Leading Negro Artists and How They Feel about Dance in the Community: Eleo Pomare, Pearl Primus and Arthur Mitchell." *Dance Magazine* (Nov. 1968): 45.

474. "Ex-Wife in Tribute to Robinson." *Boston Post* (Nov. 28, 1949).

475. Evans, Orrin C. "John Long, Long Slim Figure, Long Exponent of Dance, Dies." *Washington Tribune* (Mar. 9, 1935).

    Obituary of a dancing master of formal dances such as the waltz, gavotte, and schottische.

476. "An Example of Success in Harlem: Savoy Ballroom, Home of Happy Feet." In *Negro Anthology, 1931-1933* edited by Nancy Cunard, 323-24. London: Wishart, 1934.

477. "Exciting Ballet from Negro Company." *Edinburgh Evening News* (Sept. 24, 1957).

    Reviews the New York Negro Ballet performing in Edinburgh.

478. [F., I.M.] I.M.F. "Meanwhile Backstage." *Boston Phoenix* (Mar. 23, 1982).

    The Boston Ballet fires black South African Augustus Van Heerden.

479. Ferguson, Otis. "Breakfast Dance in Harlem." *New Republic* 86 (Feb. 12, 1936): 15-16.

    Describes a Harlem dance hall and its activity. Probably refers to the Savoy, although the name is not given.

480. Ficocella, Jane. "Morse Donaldson's Dance Company, Riverside Church Theatre, N.Y.C., March 1-4, 1972." *Dance News* (May 1972): 7

481. "First All-Negro Ballet Makes Debut in Harlem November 21." *New York Herald Tribune* (Oct. 27, 1937).

Profiles Eugene Von Grona and the forming of the American Negro Ballet.

482. "First Negro Classic Ballet." *Hue* (June 2, 1954): 12-14.

483. Fischer-Munstermann. *Jazz Dance and Jazz Gymnastics Including Disco Dancing.* Introduction by Liz Williamson. New York: Sterling Publishing Co., 1978.

Mainly a book of photographs illustrating the techniques of jazz dance. Liz Williamson's introduction gives a sketchy history.

484. Fisher, Marjory M. "Negro Ballet Wins Praise." *San Francisco News* (Aug. 16, 1952).

Reviews Hollywood Negro Ballet.

485. "Five More Years on His Toes Take Five More Off His Age." *New York Herald Tribune* (Sept. 24, 1939).

Discusses Bill Robinson's health and diet.

486. Flatow, Sheryl. "Balanchine Honored by Harlem Dance Troupe." *News World* (Feb. 25, 1979).

Reviews an all-Balanchine evening performed by the Dance Theatre of Harlem. The works danced: "Bugaku," "Agon," "Allegro Brillante," and "Four Temperaments."

487. ———. "'Holberg Suite' Showcases DTH Classic Style." *News World* (Jan. 23, 1980).

Reviews the Dance Theatre of Harlem's performance of "Holberg Suite," "Mirage," "Don Quixote pas de déux," and "Four Temperaments."

488. Fleisher, Sylvia H. "Carib Muse." Parts 1-3. *Dance Magazine* 9 (Aug., Sept., Oct. 1947): 22-27; 26, 47; 33-35.

Describes the major dances of Cuba, Dominica, and Trinidad. Also gives origins and customs surrounding them.

489. Fletcher, Tom. *100 Years of the Negro in Show Business*. New York: Burdge, 1954.

Historical and biographical information on minstrel, vaudeville, and other theatrical entertainers is combined with Tom Fletcher's own reminiscences. There are chapters on the cakewalk, Bill "Bojangles" Robinson, and Billy Kersands.

490. Flint, Timothy. *Recollections of the Last Ten Years Passed in Occasional Residences and Journeying in the Valley of the Mississippi*. Boston: Cumings, Hilliard, 1826. Reprint. George R. Brooks, ed. Carbondale, Ill.:

Includes a description of the King of the Wake ceremonies and black dancing in New Orleans.

491. Floyd, Charlotte. "Dance D.C. Dance." *The Feet* (June 1973): 13-15.

Gives a history of the D.C. Black Repertory Dance Company, with short biographies of Mike Malone and Louis Johnson, co-directors of the company.

492. "Folklore and Ethnology." *Southern Workman* 25 (Apr. 1986): 82.

Describes a Va. foot wash ritual followed by a "shout."

493. "Fontaine Dancers." *Our World* (Apr. 1953): 64-65.

494. "Former Ailey Star Becomes Teacher at Georgia State." *Jet* (Sept. 27, 1982): 38.

Sara Yarborough.

495.   Fortier, Alcée. *Louisiana Studies: Literature, Customs, Dialects, History and Education.* New Orleans: F.F. Hansell & Bro., 1894.

Part 2, "Customs and Dialects," offers descriptions of Christmas balls in La., the carabiné, pilé chactas, and the cane-cutting ceremony.

496.   Foster, George G. *New York by Gas Light.* New York: DeWitt and Davenport, 1850.

Describes blacks dancing in a dance-house called "Dicken's Place."

497.   Franck, Ruth and Linda Locke. "Observations on Negro and White Dance." *Dance Observer* (Aug.-Sept. 1944): 80-81.

These observations were made after seeing the performances of the Dance Groups of North Carolina College for Negroes and the Dance Club of the University of North Carolina. The observers found restraint in emotional expression and group-oriented movement among the blacks. The white dancers were individually more expressive. Humor was more subtle in the black group and more bold and obvious in the white group.

498.   Frank, Henry. "A Survey of Haitian Vodun Ritual Dance." *Caribe* 7 (nos. 1 & 2): 39-40.

499.   Fraser, C. Gerald. "2 Shows with Roots in Africa." *New York Times* (Aug. 13, 1982).

Discusses the importance of the African elements of religion and culture still evident in Brazil and Cuba, along with a description of capoeira, in the announcement of a forthcoming performance of Loremil Machado and his Afro-Brazilian Dance Company and Robert Borrell y su Kubata at the Lincoln Center Out of Doors Festival.

500.   Fraser, John. "Solomons and Troupe Display Art and Wit." *The Globe and Mail* [Toronto] (Oct. 17, 1973).

Reviews a performance of Gus Solomons, Jr. and his troupe at York University in Toronto.

501. Frazier, George. "A Sense of Style." *Esquire* 68, no. 5 (1967): 70-78.

Discusses black-American style in sports, dress, and dance.

502. Freeman, William M. "Ann Pennington, Dancing Star, Dies." *New York Times* (Nov. 5, 1971).

The obituary of Ann Pennington with a brief comment on the origin of the black bottom, which Pennington introduced on Broadway.

503. Fressola, Michael. "Thompson Troupe in Spring Rites." *Staten Island Advance* (May 21, 1982).

Reviews the first performance of the Clive Thompson Dance Company.

504. Frich, Elisabeth. *Matt Mattox Book of Jazz Dance.* New York: Sterling Publishing Co., Inc., 1983.

Jazz dance technique in photographs.

505. Fried, Alexander. "The Black Dancer in S.F." *San Francisco Sunday Examiner and Chronicle* (May 9, 1976).

Gives a history of the black dancer in San Francisco and announces the documentary exhibit "The Black Dancer on the San Francisco Stage" held at the Archives for the Performing Arts, Presidio Branch of the San Francisco Public Library, June 2-July 31, 1976.

506. Friedenthal, Albert. *Musik, Tanz und Dichtung bei den Kreolan Amerikas.* Berlin: H. Schnippel, 1913.

507. Friedland, Lee Ellen. "Disco: Afro-American Vernacular
Performance." *Dance Research Journal* 15, no. 2 (Spring
1983): 27-35.

Explores "the interrelationship of vernacular performance
genres and the interface between community and public culture."
Based on fieldwork in an urban black community in Philadelphia.

508. "Frisco's Joyous Dance Master." *Ebony* (Mar. 1958): 38-40.

Zack Thompson teaches ballet, modern, etc. in San Francisco.

509. Frost, Helen. *Clog and Character Dances.* New York: A.S.
Barnes, 1931.

Includes four black character dances: "Swanee," "In the
Cornfield," "Mammy," and "Jockey."

510. Frucht, Bill. "'The Big Apple': How New York Got Its Name."
Wisdom's Child (July 19, 1977).

Also describes the dance, the big apple.

511. "Funeral Rites Are Held for Nyas Berry." *New York Amsterdam
News* (Oct. 13, 1951): 1.

512. Gaines, Eddie. "Garroway Shows Philly's Art, Talented Dancers
to the Nation." *Philadelphia Afro-American* (Feb. 25, 1956).

Joe Nash and an all-black ensemble appeared on Dave
Garroway's "Today" television salute to Philadelphia, the first time
an all-black dance group was used on a Philadelphia station for
national television.

513. Gardel, Luis D. *Escola de Samba, an Effective Account of the
Carnival Guilds of Rio de Janeiro.* Rio de Janeiro: Livraria
Komos Editôra, 1967.

Gives the history, development, and organization of the
Escolas de Samba. Includes the history of the samba as a dance
and the history of the carnival in Rio.

514. Garland, Robert. "Native African Opera Proves Entertaining." *New York World-Telegram* (May 19, 1934).

Reviews Asadata Dafora's opening of "Kykunkor."

515. Gaye, Pamela Diane. "The Legacy of the Minstrel Show." *Dance Scope* 12, no. 2 (Spring/Summer 1978): 34-45.

Relates the history of black participation in minstrelsy and the stereotypes it promoted. States that minstrelsy served as a bridge to eventual serious acceptance of blacks as artists.

516. Gayle, Stephen. "Two Sophisticated Ladies Are a Smash on Broadway." *Essence* (Sept. 1981): 12-14.

Profiles singer Phyllis Hyman and dancer Judith Jamison, both stars of the Broadway hit *Sophisticated Ladies*.

517. Gelb, Arthur. "Habitues of Meyer Davis Land Dance the Twist." *New York Times* (Oct. 19, 1961).

518. Genné, Beth. "Tap Dance from Harlem." *Dancing Times* (Dec. 1980): 166-68.

Summarizes and reviews "No Maps on My Taps," the cinematic celebration of three American tap dancers: Bunny Briggs, Howard (Sandman) Sims, and Chuck Green. Also reviews a performance by those three at the Riverside Studios, London, in Oct. 1980.

519. Genovese, Eugene D. *Roll, Jordan, Roll: The World the Slaves Made.* New York: Pantheon Books, 1974.

Argues that the slaves contributed to the development of black culture and black national consciousness while contributing to American culture. To support the argument, he relates the history of slave life in the South. Includes descriptions of ring shouts (pp. 233-34), slave parties, and the dance practices of the slave master (pp. 569-73).

520.   Gent, George. "Israeli Dancers Return to City Center." *New York Times* (Dec. 5, 1972): 58.

Reviews the Batsheva Dance Company directed by William Louther.

521.   "Geoffrey Holder and Company, 92nd Street Y, November 1, 1959." *Dance Magazine* (Dec. 1959): 104.

Review.

522.   Ghent, Henri. "Dance Theatre of Harlem: A Study of Triumph over Adversity." *Crisis* (July 1980): 199-202.

523.   Gilbert, Douglas. "Bill Robinson's Success Due in Part to Marty Forkins, Not to Mention Shirley Temple." *New York World-Telegram* (Nov. 12, 1940).

Forkins was Robinson's manager for 40 years.

524.   Gilbert, Morris. "Up and Coming—Janet Collins, the Met's Prima Ballerina Started Her Dancing A, B, C's." *New York Times Magazine* (Feb. 1, 1953).

525.   Gilbert, Will G. *...Rumbamuziek.* Gravenhage: J. Philip Kruseman, [1945].

Describes some dance, but is mainly about music.

526.   Giordano, Gus, ed. *Anthology of American Jazz Dance, 1975.* Evanston, Ill.: Orion Publishing House, 1975.

Divided into three parts. Part 1 is an anthology consisting of chronologically arranged reprints of articles appearing in major periodicals. The articles include reviews, criticism, histories of jazz dance, groups, and performers. Part 2 contains photos of jazz dancers. Part 3 is a jazz class with floor and barre stretches, port de bras, and combinations for beginning, intermediate, and advanced students. A dictionary and index are included.

527. "Girl with Talent to Burn." *Hue* (Jan. 1956): 23-25.

Angela Davila of New York City.

528. Gleason, Ralph J. *"Jazz Dance*, a Remarkable Book." *New York Post* (Dec. 10, 1968).

Review of Marshall Stearns's *Jazz Dance*.

529. Goddard, Chris. *Jazz Away from Home.* New York and London: Paddington Press, 1979.

Examines how and when jazz reached Europe. Chapter 2 discusses theater and dance.

530. Goffman, Kimbal. "Black Pride." *Atlantic Monthly* 163, no. 2 (Feb. 1939): 235-41.

Observes the originality of black expression in music and dance. Mentions the charleston, Suzie Q., and the big apple. Does not, however, describe these dances.

531. Goines, Margaretta Bobo. "African Retentions in the Dance of the Americas." In *Dance Research Monograph One* , 207-29. New York: CORD, 1973.

Emphasizes black dance in Latin America and the Caribbean, areas where, in the author's opinion, the greatest number of African retentions exist. She discusses the place of dance in African society and lists the specific characteristics of such dance. She covers African retentions in the dances of Haiti, Cuba, Surinam, Brazil, and the United States. Some of the specific dances are ring dances, dancing in Congo Square, social dances in the United States, and religious dances, capoeira, maculele, and the samba in Brazil.

532. Goldman, Albert. "The World's Wildest Music Festival." *Travel and Leisure* (Feb.-Mar. 1972): 57-60.

Describes the carnival in Rio de Janeiro.

533. Goldner, Nancy. "Making the Past Fresh." *Christian Science Monitor* (Jan. 17, 1980).

Reviews the Dance Theatre of Harlem's "Swan Lake" and "Paquita" during its tenth anniversary season.

534. ———. "Harlem Dance Theater: The One that Had Paris Swooning." *Christian Science Monitor* (Jan. 13, 1981).

Reviews Dance Theatre of Harlem's production of "Scheherazade."

535. ———. "Ballets that Tell a Story." *Christian Science Monitor* (Jan. 26, 1982).

Reviews Dance Theatre of Harlem's rendition of Valerie Bettis' "A Streetcar Named Desire" and John Taras' "Firebird."

536. ———. "Harlem Dance Troupe Mixes Spice, Fascination." *Christian Science Monitor* (Feb. 14, 1983).

Reviews some of the Dance Theatre of Harlem's repertory: "Les Biches," "Scheherazade," and "Frankie and Johnny."

537. "The Gombey Dance." *Dancing Times* (Dec. 1938): 275-76.

Describes the rhythms, costumes, and steps of the dance done in the West Indies on Christmas and Boxing Day.

538. Gonzalez-Wippler, Migene. *The Santería Experience.* Englewood Cliffs, N.J.: Prentice-Hall, 1982.

The Puerto Rican-born author relates personal experiences of her participation in the religion of Santería and describes some of the ceremonial dances.

539. "Goodbye to Bojangles." *Life* (Dec. 12, 1949).

540. Goodwin, Noël. "Black Octave: Eight New Works from Alvin Ailey's American Dance Theater at the Edinburgh Festival, August 1968." *Dance and Dancers* (Oct. 1968): 23-30.

541. Goodwin, Ruby Berkley. "Aurora Greeley, Dancer, and Leader of Chorus of 30 Has Never Had a Love Affair." *Afro-American* (Nov. 7, 1931).

542. Goss, Wade Tynes Pretton and Julinda Lewis Williams. "A Call for Valid Dance Criticism." In *Dance Research Collage* , edited by Patricia A. Rowe and Ernestine Stodelle, 77-80. New York: CORD, 1979.

Explains and gives a history of the need for black dance criticism.

543. Graham, Alfredo. "It's the Pachanga . . . Ole! *Pittsburgh Courier* [New York Edition, Section 2] (June 10, 1961): 20.

Discusses the pachanga craze, with a diagram of the steps.

544. Greskovic, Robert. "The Dance Theatre of Harlem: A Work in Progress." *Ballet Review* 4, no. 6 (1974): 43-60.

Analyzes the company's technique and choreography from the viewpoint of the company as a work in progress.

545. Grim, George. "Who's Dora Dean?" *Minneapolis Morning Tribune* (Oct. 22, 1946).

Briefly profiles the team of Johnson and Dean, vaudevillians and champion cakewalkers.

546. Grimes, John. "Caribbean Music and Dance." *Freedomways* 4 (1964): 426-34.

Reveals that music and dance played a major part in the development of the entire West Indies.

547. Gulden, Bruce. "Louis Gruenberg's Opera 'The Emperor Jones.'" *Dance Culture* (Mar. 1933): 12.

Reviews the opera with a special mention of Hemsley Winfield's performance as the witch doctor.

548. Guy, Edna. "Negro Dance Pioneers." *Dance Herald* (Mar. 1938): 6.

Looks at three pioneers in concert dance—Katherine Dunham, Hemsley Winfield, and Edna Guy.

549. Gwynne, James. "Book Review: *Color Me White.*" *On Stage* (Apr. 1981): 7.

Autobiography of dancer Arthur Wright, who has vitiligo.

550. ———. "Larry Phillips: Profile." *On Stage* (Apr. 1981): 3, 6.

Dancer and founder of the Thelma Hill Performing Arts Center.

551. [H., A.] A.H. "Now—Ballet and Variety All in One Show." *Glasgow Evening Citizen* (Sept. 10, 1957).

Reviews the New York Negro Ballet in Glasgow.

552. [H., D.] D.H. "Donald McKayle and Company, 92nd Street Y. April 22, 1962." *Dance Magazine* (June 1962): 64.

Reviews a performance of "Rainbow 'Round My Shoulder" and "District Storyville."

553. ———. "Folk Program Given by Jamaican Group." *New York Times* (July 19, 1971).

Reviews the Jamaican Folksingers group performing at the Hunter College Assembly Hall.

554. [H., W.] W.H. "First All-Negro Classic Ballet Notably Original." *Los Angeles Times* (Feb. 26, 1951).

Reviews the Hollywood Negro Ballet, also known as the First Negro Classic Ballet.

555. Haines, Aubrey B. "Where the Tap Dance Came From." *Dance Digest* (Mar. 1958): 92.

556. "Haitian Dancer Too Rich for Club's Blood." *Afro-American* (Sept. 26, 1959): 6.

Jean-Léon Destiné's hosts are asked to resign from a private club in Norwalk, Conn. after they bring him there as their guest.

557. Haizlip, Ellis. "Ed Sullivan Must Change!" *Dance Scope* 3, no. 2 (Spring 1967): 30-34.

Haizlip speaks as the producer of Donald McKayle's "Black New World."

558. Hall, Nick J. "Black Flamenco Dancers in Spain." *Sepia* (May 1974): 66-71.

Profiles two black-American dancers who became star flamenco performers in Spain.

559. Halsell, Venetia. "Dancing to Improve One's Health." *Chicago Defender* (Mar. 14, 1979): 18.

Jimmy Payne's School of Dance in Chicago is frequented by professionals and fitness students. Payne is a long-time instructor and choreographer.

560. Hammond, Sally. "He Does the Cakewalk or Cha-Cha and It's Art." *New York Post* (June 10, 1958).

Al Minns, well-known Savoy dancer, works to preserve old jazz dances like the lindy, big apple, etc.

561. Haney, Lynn. *Naked at the Feast: A Biography of Josephine Baker*. New York: Dodd, Mead and Company, 1981.

562.   Hanna, Judith Lynne. "Functions of African and American Negro Secular Dances: Parallel Answers and Research Questions." Paper presented at the annual meeting of the African Studies Association, Nov. 1967, New York City.

563.   Hansen, Chadwick. "Jenny's Toe: Negro Shaking Dances in America." *American Quarterly* 19, no. 3 (1967): 554-63.

Discusses the tradition of hip-shaking dances of the American black and relates it to the twist and other popular dances.

564.   Happel, Richard V. "Ethnic, Ballet at Pillow." *Berkshire Eagle* (Aug. 13, 1969).

Reviews a performance of the Afro-American Dance Ensemble of Philadelphia at Jacob's Pillow.

565.   "Harlem Dance Theatre Begins Nassau Performance Tonight." *Bahamian Times* (June 24, 1970).

Reviews the Dance Theatre of Harlem in the Bahamas.

566.   "Harlem Dancers Perform in Capital." *New York Times* (Jan. 23, 1974).

Reports on a series of workshops the Dance Theatre of Harlem scheduled to present to school children at Ford's Theater in Washington, D.C.

567.   "Harlem Dancers Wow London." *Newsday* (Aug. 16, 1979).

Dance Theatre of Harlem.

568.   "Harlem under Control: Negro Ballet Gives 'Fire Bird' and Park Ave. Approves." *Newsweek* (Nov. 29, 1937): 28.

Reports on the first performance of the American Negro Ballet at the LaFayette Theatre.

569.   Harman, Carter. *The West Indies.* New York: Time, Inc., 1963.

Surveys the history and characteristics of all the West Indian islands. Describes dancing (pp. 64-67) and a voodoo ceremony (pp. 53-56).

570. Harn, Julia E. "Old Canooche-Ogache Chronicles." *Georgia Historical Quarterly* 15 (1931): 346-60; 16 (1932): 146-50, 232-40.

Mentions the influence of old black dances on the modern.

571. Harriot, Frank. "Carib Manhattan." *Mademoiselle* (Mar. 1946): 160, 271-72.

Features New Yorkers of Caribbean descent, including dancers Belle Rosette (Beryl McBurnie), Josephine Premice, and Claude Marchant.

572. Harris, Harry. "African Dances Are Offered." *Philadelphia Inquirer* (Jan. 16, 1969).
Reviews a performance of the Afro-American Dance Ensemble on WHYY-TV, Jan. 15, 1969.

573. Harrold, Robert. "The Splendid Alvin Ailey...." *Dancing Times* (May 1965): 397-98.

Reviews Alvin Ailey's second London season in Mar. 1965. The works performed: Anna Sokolow's "Rooms," Louis Johnson's "Lament," Talley Beatty's "Congo Tango Palace," and various Ailey pieces.

574. Hartley, Russell. "The Black Artist on the San Francisco Stage." *This World* [*San Francisco Chronicle*] (June 6, 1976).

History of the black dancer on the San Francisco stage.

575. Hartshorne, Joan and Tom Hartshorne. "Jolly Black Minstrels Need Not Apply." *Dance Scope* 3, no. 2 (Spring 1967): 17-22.

"A report from Karamu."

576. Haskell, Arnold Lionel. "Further Studies in Ballet." *Dancing Times* (Jan. 1930): 455-57.

Feels jazz is best danced by blacks. Whites are not as spontaneous and their jazz dances, even if performed well, are not genuine.

577. Haskins, James. *Katherine Dunham.* New York: Coward, McCann, & Geoghegan, Inc., 1982.

578. Hays, Alfreda. "The Chuck Davis Dance Company." *Independent Press* (Sept. 5, 1979).

At Drew University.

579. Hazzard-Gordon, Katrina. "Atiba's a Comin': The Rise of Social Dance Formations in Afro-American Culture." Ph.D. thesis, Cornell University, 1983.

Traces the origins and forms of black working-class cultural arenas by exploring ten contexts in which the black-American has danced: jooks, honky-tonks, after-hours joints, rent parties, dance halls, block parties, membership clubs, night clubs, quadroon balls, and elite dances.

580. ———. "Afro-American Core Culture Social Dance: An Examination of Four Aspects of Meaning." *Dance Research Journal* 15, no. 2 (Spring 1983): 21-26.

Examines four theoretical areas of black-American vernacular dance: psychological identity, political resistance, cultural integrity, and group dynamics.

581. Hearn, Lafcadio. *Two Years in the French West Indies.* New York: Harper & Brothers, 1890.

Describes the calinda, the bélé, and the musical instruments that accompany them when danced in Martinique (pp. 143-46).

582. ———. *The Life and Letters of Lafcadio Hearn* edited by Elizabeth Bisland. Boston: Houghton Mifflin, 1906.

Hearn's letters to H.E. Krehbiel discuss New Orleans and West Indian black music and its relationship to West African music and dance.

583. ———. "Banjo Jim's Story." In *An American Miscellany vol. 1* edited by Albert Mordell, 181-89. New York: Dodd, Mead, 1924.

Ghost story from New Orleans includes a description of phantom fiddlers haunting a dance.

584. ———. "Levee Life." In *An American Miscellany , vol. 1* edited by Albert Mordell, 147-70. New York: Dodd, Mead, 1924.

Describes life among black roustabouts and longshoremen; also describes juba dancing, set dances, quadrilles, and Virginia reels danced at a place called Ryan's Dance-house.

585. ———. "The Scenes of Cable's Romances." In *An American Miscellany , vol. 2* edited by Albert Mordell, 168-84. New York: Dodd, Mead, 1924.

Describes life in New Orleans and dancing in Congo Square.

586. Hellinger, Mark. "Broadway Loves Bill Robinson." *Pittsburgh Courier* (Nov. 15, 1930).

587. "Hemsley Winfield, Actor, Victim of Pneumonia." *New York Age* (Jan. 20, 1934).

Obituary.

588. Henderson, W.J. "Native African Opera Moves." *New York Sun* (May 21, 1934).

Kykunkor moves to the Chanin Building in New York City.

589.   "Henry Le Tang." *Attitude* (Sept./Oct. 1983): 21.

Profiles a long-time dance teacher of Harlem.

590.   Hentoff, Nat. *An Inheritance Comes to P.S. 83.*   Washington, D.C.: U.S. Government Printing Office, 1966. Reprinted from *American Education* (Apr. 1966).

Reports that Pearl Primus completed a portion of her doctoral requirements by giving a dance demonstration at P.S. 83 in New York City. The thesis was, "elementary school children can learn more about cultures unfamiliar to them by seeing and hearing elements of those cultures come to life in front of them."

591.   Hepburn, D. "Brown Legs Return to Broadway." *Sepia* (Jan. 1960): 61-65.

The night club Copper Door attempts to bring a "permanent brown-skinned chorus line" back to Broadway.   Clarence Robinson produced the show that included Joel Nobel as choreographer, the Step Brothers, and Cab Calloway.

592.   Herbert, Robert. "Essence Women: Marie Brooks." *Essence* (Sept. 1977): 14.

Biography of the founder of Marie Brooks Children's Dance-Research Theatre.

593.   Herring, Doris. "The Workshop, a New Perennial." *Dance Magazine* (July 1947): 19-21.

The Choreographer's Workshop concert features Talley Beatty's "Southern Landscape (1865)."

594.   ———. "Helen McGehee and Ronne Aul. *Dance Magazine* (June 1951): 11, 45.

Reviews a joint recital at the YW-YMHA, Apr. 7, 1951.

Pearl Primus   *Unknown*

Voodoo Dance   *Illustration from Harpers Weekly*

Alvin Ailey American Dance Theater   *Unknown*
Schomburg Center for Research in Black Culture
The New York Public Library
Astor, Lenox and Tilden Foundations

Tap Dancers from a Night Club Production   *Unknown*
Schomburg Center for Research in Black Culture
The New York Public Library
Astor, Lenox and Tilden Foundations

International Afrikan American Ballet *Sule Gregg Wilson*
Schomburg Center for Research in Black Culture
The New York Public Library
Astor, Lenox and Tilden Foundations

Lindy Hoppers at the Savoy   *Unknown*
Schomburg Center for Research in Black Culture
The New York Public Library
Astor, Lenox and Tilden Foundations

595. ———. Donald McKayle and Co.; Pauline Koner and Co.; John Butler Dance Theatre 92nd St. 'Y' March 23, 1958." *Dance Magazine* (May 1958): 25, 26, 65.

596. ———. "Louis Johnson and Company. 92nd Street 'Y' March 9, 1958." *Dance Magazine* (May 1958): 25.

597. ———. "Jean-Leon Destiné and His Haitian Dance Co." *Dance Magazine* (July 1958): 77-78.

598. ———. "Carmina Burana: New York City Opera." *Dance Magazine* (Nov. 1959): 60-61.

599. ———. Review of "Black New World" by Donald McKayle at the 92nd St. Y., Feb. 8, 1967. *Dance Magazine* (Apr. 1967): 34.

600. ———. "Why Ohio? A Dance Safari through the Buckeye State." *Dance Magazine* (Sept. 1971): 48-62.

Discusses dance activity throughout Ohio, including Cleveland's Karamu House Dance Department.

601. Herridge, Frances. "The Tragic Mute of the 'Medium.' *PM* (Aug. 31, 1947).

Reviews Leo Coleman in Gian Carlo Menotti's opera.

602. ———. "Beating Delinquency with Heel and Toe." *PM* (July 4, 1948).

Profiles Mary Bruce and her dance school coping with delinquency in Harlem.

603. ———. "Across the Footlights: Holder and Amaya in Central Park." *New York Post* (June 18, 1957).

Reviews Geoffrey Holder dancing his "Banda," "Dougla," and "Bélé" with Carmen De Lavallade.

604. ———. "Modern Dancer Joins American Ballet Group." *New York Post* (Jan. 26, 1966): 60.

Reviews Mary Hinkson and Scott Douglas premièring in Glen Tetley's "Ricercare."

605. ———. "Talley Beatty Work at ANTA." *New York Post* (Apr. 19, 1974): 36.

Dance Theatre of Harlem premières Talley Beatty's "Caravansarai."

606. ———. "Christian Holder Debut in Joffrey Ballet Repertory." *New York Post* (Oct. 17, 1975).

607. ———. "Rod Rodgers: Half a Treat." *New York Post* (Nov. 11, 1976).

Reviews the Rod Rodgers Dance Company.

608. ———. "Clothes Do Not the Dancer Make." *New York Post* (Dec. 8, 1976).

Reviews Dudley Williams in Alvin Ailey's "Love Songs."

609. ———. "Harlem Offers Two Premières." *New York Post* (Feb. 28, 1979).

Reviews two Dance Theatre of Harlem premières, "Serenade" and "Mirage." "Manifestations" and "Troy Game" were also performed

610. Herskovits, Melville J. and Frances S. Herskovits. *Rebel Destiny: Among the Bush Negroes of Dutch Guiana.* New York: Whittlesey House, 1934.

Chapter 1, "Death at Gankwe," describes Kromanti dancing at a funeral ceremony. Chapter 18, "Obia Comes (pp. 322-40), describes an Obia ceremony with dancing.

611. Herskovits, Melville J. *Life in a Haitian Valley.* New York: Knopf, 1937.

Investigates everyday life in the valley of Mirebalais. Describes voodoo dances (pp. 189-98) and the characteristics of Haitian dances (pp. 262-64).

612. —— and Frances S. Herskovits. *Trinidad Village.* New York: Knopf, 1947.

This ethnographic study of a Trinidad village does not describe dances themselves, but does show their purpose and place in the rituals and life of the village. Dances discussed: bongo, reel, bélé, Shango cult dancing, quadrille, passé, and jig.

613. Herskovits, Melville J. *The New World Negro.* Bloomington, Ind.: Indiana University Press, 1966.

These selected papers present a survey of the author's study of blacks in the Western Hemisphere. Dances are mentioned within the context of the various cultures studied.

614. Hieronymous, Clara. "Fat Tuesday Dips Generous Portion." *The Tennessean* (Feb. 11, 1977).

Reviews "Fat Tuesday (and All that Jazz)" performed by the Arthur Hall Afro-American Dance Ensemble at the Tennessee Arts Foundation in Nashville.

615. Highwater, Jamake. "Dancing in the Seventies." *Horizon* 19, no. 3 (May 1977): 30-33.

Discusses the development of the disco dance craze of the 1970s, showing similarities to and differences from rock dancing of the 1960s and how blacks have influenced the dancing patterns of white Americans through Elvis Presley. Also includes a brief biography of Snake Hips Tucker.

616.   Hill, Thelma. "Where Hate Is Not the Answer." *Dance Scope* 3, no. 2 (Spring 1967): 35-37.

Reports on the work of the Dance Division of Haryou.

617.   Hitchins, Aubrey. "Creating the Negro Dance Theatre." *Dance and Dancers* (Apr. 1956): 12-13.

The founding of the all-male company.

618.   Hobson, Charles. "The Living Arts." *Tuesday Magazine* (Feb. 1972): 4.

Reviews Ailey's "Mary Lou's Mass" with a brief comment on Ailey's career.

619.   ———. "Deborah Allen: A Serious Young Actress." *Black Stars* (Sept. 1974): 32-35.

620.   Holder, Geoffrey. "The Twist? 'It's Not a Dance.'" *New York Times Magazine* (Dec. 3, 1961): 78.

621.   ———. "The Night They Killed the Bossa Nova." *Saturday Review* (Oct. 12, 1963).

622.   Hollenweger, Walter J. "Danced Documentaries: The Theological and Political Significance of Pentecostal Dancing." In *Worship and Dance* edited by J. G. Davies, pp. 76-82. Birmingham, England: University of Birmingham, 1975.

Discusses black Pentecostal churches in the United States, their dances, liturgy, and political freedom.

623.   "Hollywood Picks George Davis as Favorite Dancer." *Chicago Defender* (May 24, 1958): 18.

Davis is picked to play in a film version of the life of Bill Robinson.

624. Holmes, Isaac. *An Account of the United States of America, Derived from Actual Observation, During a Residence of Four Years in that Republic.* London: H. Fisher, [1823].

Describes Congo dancing and musical instruments of rural Mississippi and Louisiana (p. 332) and quadroon balls of New Orleans (p. 333).

625. Honorat, Michel Lamartine. *Les Danses Folkloriques Haitiennes.* Port-au-Prince: Imprimerie de l'Etat, 1955.

Classifies and describes Haitian folk dances individually. Gives a history of Haitian folk dancing as well as descriptions and use of musical instruments, songs, and costumes. Bibliography.

626. Horne, Joan. "Opener at Orpheum Revives Beale Spirit." *Commercial Appeal* [Memphis] (Feb. 18, 1977).

Reviews the Arthur Hall Afro-American Dance Ensemble dancing "Fat Tuesday (and All that Jazz)."

627. Hornsey, Jana Czernitska. "Pearl Primus, Her Adventures in and out of Africa Take a Happy Turn." *Dance Magazine* (Feb. 1962): 36-37, 52.

Discusses an impending Pearl Primus dance tour of Africa that would organize and plan dance performances adding local artists to the Primus company. She and her husband wanted to create centers in each country to preserve and teach African ritual dances in danger of extinction.

628. Horosko, Marian. "Tap, Tapping, and Tappers." *Dance Magazine* 45 (Oct. 1971): 32-37.

Relates the history of tap dancing and interviews Buddy Bradley and Bert Gibson.

629. "Hot Taps and Cool Songs." *Hue* (Feb. 1955): 53-55.

> Ken Barry, 13 years old, is hailed as a budding Sammy Davis, Jr.

630. Hughes, Allen. "Dance: Alvin Ailey Is Victor over Rain." *New York Times* (Sept. 10, 1962).

> On a rainy night at the Delacorte Theatre in Central Park, Ailey's company performed the following: "Been Here and Gone," "Roots of the Blues," "Revelations," and "Creation of the World."

631. ———. "'Unprecedented' Challenge: Staging a Bernstein Mass." *New York Times* (Aug. 24, 1971).

> Gordon Davidson and Alvin Ailey discuss their staging of the Bernstein Mass for the John F. Kennedy Center for the Performing Arts in Washington, D.C.

632. Hughes, Langston and Milton Meltzer. *Black Magic: A Pictorial History of the Negro in American Entertainment.* Englewood Cliffs, N.J.: Prentice-Hall, 1967.

> Covers dance-related subjects such as "The Minstrels" (pp. 20-32), "Bert Williams" (p. 54), "T.O.B.A." (p. 67), "Happy Feet" (dancing in the 1920s, pp. 91-96), and "Dancers and Dancing" ("serious dance") covering such dancers as Katherine Dunham and Pearl Primus (pp. 264-67).

633. Hunter, Robert G. "The Hoofers Are No More." *Negro Digest* (Feb. 1965): 82-87.

> Profiles Bill Robinson's career and discusses the demise of tap dancing as an art.

634. Hunter-Gault, Charlayne. "'African Goddess' from Philly." *New York Times* (Nov. 19, 1972).

> Profiles Judith Jamison.

635.   Hurd, Dedra. "The Black Dance Workshop of Buffalo." *The Feet* (June 1973): 12, 31.

Reviews the performance of "Mumblings: Our Women" at the Negro Ensemble Company Dance and Music Festival.

636.   Hurston, Zora Neale. "Dance Songs and Tales from the Bahamas." *Journal of American Folk-lore* 43 (July-Oct. 1930): 294-312.

Describes two forms of the Bahamian fire dance along with the songs that accompany it. The second part of the article has folk tales.

637.   ———. "Characteristics of Negro Expression." In *Negro Anthology, 1931-1933* edited by Nancy Cunard, 39-46. London: Wishart, 1934.

Discusses black expression in a series of short essays on drama, speech, dancing, culture heroes, and the jook.

638.   ———. *Tell My Horse.* Berkeley, Calif.: Turtle Island, 1981.

Recounts her travels to Jamaica and Haiti. Describes Pocomania wedding and funeral customs. Also extensively discusses voodoo.

639.   Hyppolite, Michelson Paul. *A Study of Haitian Folklore.* Translated by Edgar LaForest. Port-au-Prince: Imprimerie de l'Etat, 1954.

These lectures given at the Alliance Française of Jamaica on Nov. 8 and 14, 1952 discuss Haiti and the development and practice of voodoo, including the dances. Describes the zépaules, yanvallou, mahi, banda, and congo.

640.   Iachetta, Michael. "M'Kayle Work in N.Y. Bow." *New York News* (Oct. 17, 1972).

Reviews the première of "Sojourn" danced by Donald McKayle's Inner City Repertory Dance Company.

641. Ianni, Octavio. "O Samba No Terreiro de Itú." *Revista de História*
        [São Paulo] 12, no. 26 (1956): 403.

642. "Irish Mornings and African Days on the Old Minstrel Stage: An
        Interview with Leni Sloan." *Callahan's Irish Quarterly* , no. 2
        (Spring 1982): 49-53.

        Discusses the background of early minstrel shows, including
the dances performed.

643. Isaacs, Edith J[uliet] R[ich]. *The Negro in the American Theatre.*
        New York: Theatre Arts, Inc., 1947.

        A history of blacks in the American theater, including the
history of minstrels. Mentions major black dancers such as Bill
Robinson, Asadata Dafora, Pearl Primus, Katherine Dunham,
Toneea Massaquoi (Frank Roberts), and Josephine Baker.

644. "Ismay Andrews Dancer, Died at Age 75." *New York Amsterdam
        News* (Mar. 23, 1975): B7.

645. [J., H.] H.J. "Talley Beatty and Company." *Dance Observer* 15
        (Nov. 1948): 122.

        Reviews a concert at the YW-YMHA, New York City, Oct. 24,
1948. The dances performed: "Rural Dances of Cuba," "Southern
Landscape," "Saudades do Brazil," "Blues," and "Kanzo."

646. [J., L.] L.J. "Geoffrey Holder: One-Man Museum Plans a
        Museum." *Dance Magazine* (May 1954): 18.

        Holder plans for a Caribbean museum in New York City.

647. Jackson, Fay M. "Movie Stars at Birthday Fete for Him."
        Chicago Defender (June 15, 1935).

        Bill Robinson's birthday.

648. Jackson, Harriet. "American Dancer, Negro." *Dance Magazine* 40 (Sept. 1966): 35-42.

Surveys black dance from Africa to the United States and modern times. The topics covered: minstrel dances, tap and jazz dancing, ballet, and modern dance.

649. Jackson, Irene V. *Afro-American Religious Music.* Westport, Conn.: Greenwood Press, 1979.

This bibliography includes the chapter "Ethnomusicology, Dance, Folklore," pp. 8-13.

650. Jackson, Martin A. "For Gregory Hines, the Uncertainty Is Over." *Encore American and Worldwide News* (Nov. 1981): 28-31.

651. "Jam Session in Movie Land." *Ebony* (Nov. 1945): 6-9.

About the filming of Gjon Mili's "Jammin' the Blues."

652. "Jamaica Dances to John Canoe." *New York Herald Tribune* (Nov. 10, 1957): 10.

653. James, Willis Laurence. "The Romance of the Negro Folk Cry in America." *Phylon* 16, no. 1 (1955): 15-30.

How folk cries are used, including their use in dances.

654. "Janet Collins." *Afro-American* , Magazine Section (Nov. 29, 1952): 1, 10.

655. "Janet Collins, Ballerina at the Met." *Color* (June 1952): 42.

656. Jattefaux, Maurice. *Apprenons à Danser.* Paris: Libraire Garnier Frères [1934].

Gives dance steps to the charleston, black bottom, tango, samba, and fox trot.

657. "'Jazz Dance' on Film." *New York Times Magazine* (Sept. 5, 1954).

Photo story about the film by Roger Tilton.

658. *Jazzdans*. Brevskolan: n.p., 1973.

This photographic book on jazz techniques discusses the history of black dance in "Jazz dansens ursprung" (pp. 73-97).

659. Jensen, Gregory. "Harlem Ballet Delights Large London Crowds." *Staten Island Advance* (Aug. 15, 1979).

Dance Theatre of Harlem.

660. "Jimmy Mordecai Is Dead." *New York Amsterdam News* (May 7, 1966): 1.

Mordecai performed with the dance team of Mordecai, Wells and Taylor.

661. "Jody (Butter Beans) Edwards, Comedian, Dancer, Singer, Dies." *New York Times* (Oct. 30, 1967).

Obituary gives a profile of Edwards's career.

662. "Joel Hall Dancers." *Attitude* 2, no. 6 (Nov. 1983): 16.

Profiles the company.

663. Johns, Vere E. "In the Name of Art." *New York Age* (Jan. 27, 1934).

Obituary of Hemsley Winfield.

664. Johnson, Carole. "Reflections on 'Organization' in the Dance World." *The Feet* (June 1973): 26.

Addresses the issue of organizing black dance and discusses the role that the Modern Organization for Dance Evolvement

(M.O.D.E.) plays in meeting the needs of dancers, companies, and schools.

665. Johnson, Greer. "Jacob's Pillow Dance Festival." *Cue* (Aug. 30, 1969).

Reviews the Afro-American Dance Ensemble at Jacob's Pillow.

666. Johnson, Gregory. "Harlem Ballet Delights Large London Crowds." *Staten Island Advance* (Aug. 15, 1979).

Dance Theatre of Harlem.

667. Johnson, Helen Armstead. "Blacks in Vaudeville: Broadway and Beyond." In *American Popular Entertainment: Papers and Proceedings of the Conference on the History of American Popular Entertainment* edited by Myron Matlaw, 77-86. Westport, Conn.: Greenwood Press, 1979.

Reflects on the history of blacks in vaudeville and illustrates their influence on white performers.

668. Johnson, Herschel. "The New Generation and the Arts." *Ebony* (Aug. 1978): 149-51.

Features several rising dancers such as Debbie Allen, Ed Love, Virginia Johnson, and Ronald Perry.

669. Johnson, James Weldon. *Black Manhattan.* New York: Knopf, 1930.

History of blacks in New York that includes discussion of early drama and musical theater, dance, sports, parades, night life, etc.

670. Johnson, Thomas A. "I Must Be Black and Do Black Things." *New York Times* (Sept. 7, 1969).

Eleo Pomare comments on his works.

671. Jolicoeur, Aubelin. "La Grande Danseuse Lavinia Williams." *Le Nouvelliste* (June 20, 1953).

672. Jones, Bessie and Bess Lomax Hawes. *Step It Down: Games, Plays, Songs, and Stories from the Afro-American Heritage.* New York: Harper & Row, 1972.

Gives texts and music of baby games, clapping plays, jumps and skips, singing plays, ring plays, dances, house plays, outdoor games, songs, tales, and riddles. Dances featured in Chapter 6 are possum-la, ranky tank, coonshine, sandy ree, zudie-o, I'm going away to see Aunt Dinah, and Daniel.

673. Jones, Duane L. and Joanne Robinson. "*Caribe* Interview with Rex Nettleford." *Caribe* 7, nos. I & II: 24-28.

674. Jones, Duane L. "Dance Black America." *Caribe* 7, nos. I & II: 50-52.

Review.

675. ———. "Interview with Fradique Lizardo." *Caribe* 7, nos. I & II: 44-46.

Lizardo is with Ballet Folklorico Dominicano.

676. Jones, John Hudson. "Saga of Negro Dancer William 'Bill' Bailey." *Daily Worker* (Apr. 11, 1951).

Bill Bailey makes a comeback performance with Count Basie after eight years of preaching.

677. Jones, Paula. "The American Dance Stage Is Still Dominated by Jim Crow." *Daily Worker* (Apr. 8, 1952).

678. Jones, William H. *Recreation and Amusement among Negroes in Washington, D.C.; A Sociological Analysis of the Negro in an Urban Environment.* Washington, D.C.: Howard University Press, 1927.

Has chapters on cabarets and dance halls.

679. Jorio, Amaury. *Escolas de Samba Em Desfile; Vida, Paixão e Sorte.* N.p: Poligráfica Editora, Ltda., 1969.

680. "Josephine Baker, Toast of Paris." *Michigan Chronicle* (Feb. 20, 1982): A-2.

681. Jowitt, Deborah. "Better Mouse Traps." *Village Voice* (June 4, 1970).

Reviews the Ron Davis Dancers from the Johnson C. Smith University performing at Alice Tully Hall in New York City.

682. ———. "The Solomons Company." *Village Voice* (June 20, 1974).

Reviews Gus Solomons, Jr. and his company at the American Theater Lab, New York City.

683. ———. "Call Me a Dancer." *New York Times Magazine* (Dec. 5, 1976): 40-41, 136-43, 148.

Profiles Judith Jamison.

684. ———. "Old Triumphs Revisited." *Village Voice* (Jan. 28, 1980): 69.

Reviews Dance Theatre of Harlem's "Swan Lake, Act II" and "Greening" at City Center, New York City.

685. Joyaux, Georges J. "Forest's Voyage aux États Unis de l'Amérique en 1831." *Louisiana Historical Quarterly* 39 (Oct. 1956): 457-72.

An extract from P. Forest's travelogue describes the blacks from New Orleans gathering on Sundays at a place called The Camp where dances were held.

686. "Judith Jamison 'Call Me a Dancer.'" *Ebony* (Aug. 1977): 135.

687.   "K. Dunham's 'La Boule Blanche.'" *New York Amsterdam News* (July 10, 1948): 7.

Katherine Dunham sponsors monthly sessions of La Boule Blanche in New York.

688.   [K., I.] I.K.   "Negro Ballet Has Performance." *New York Sun* (Nov. 22, 1937).

Reviews the debut of the American Negro Ballet.

689.   ———.   "Two Companies Dance." *New York Sun* (Mar. 21, 1938).

Reviews the performance of the American Negro Ballet in a benefit for the New York Urban League.

690.   [K., N.] N.K.   "Hadassah and Claude Marchant." *Dance Observer* 14, no. 3 (Mar. 1947): 30.

Reviews a shared program at the 92nd St. "Y.," Feb. 12, 1947.

691.   ———.   "Books: *Isles of Rhythm* by Earl Leaf." *Dance Observer* 15 (Nov. 1948): 123.

Book review.

692.   Kahn, Morton C.   "Notes on the Saramaccaner Bush Negroes of Dutch Guiana." *American Anthropologist* 31 (1929): 468-90.

Describes Bandamba and Oggaloosa dances (p. 485).

693.   [Karamu Dancers at the World's Fair.] *New York Times* (July 21, 1940).

Announcement of a forthcoming appearance of the Karamu Dancers with a brief history of the company.

694.   "Kathe Sandler Makes Film about Thelma Hill." *New York Amsterdam News* (Oct. 16, 1982): 24.

695. "Katherine Dunham." *Caribe* 7, nos. I & II: 13.

Biographical sketch.

696. "Katherine Dunham." *Crisis* (June 1950): 344.

697. "Katherine Dunham: Ambassador with Hips." *Our World* (Sept. 1950): 42-44.

Illustrates Katherine Dunham's popularity with audiences, anthropological societies and diplomats in Mexico and Europe.

698. "Katherine Dunham Pioneers: Celebration of Women Dancers." *New York Amsterdam News* (Jan. 24, 1981).

Announces a program to honor sixteen female dancers from Dunham's first dance company to be held at the Thelma Hill Performing Arts Center.

699. "Katherine Dunham Spices Up Dance Revue." *Ebony* (Aug. 1955): 25-27.

700. "Katherine Dunham's New Show." *Sepia* (Nov. 1962): 71-74.

The show entitled "Bamboche" tours the United States.

701. Kaufman, Bill. "Ben Vereen Kicks and Croons in Special." *Staten Island Advance* (Feb. 26, 1978).

702. Kavanagh, Julie. "Pas de Decor." *Times Literary Supplement* (July 4, 1980).

Reviews Dance Theatre of Harlem's performance at London's Sadler's Wells Theatre. Works performed: "Troy Game," "Holberg Suite," "Adagietto No. 5," "Four Temperaments."

703. Kealiinohomoku, Joann Wheeler. "Ethnic Historical Study." In *Dance History Research: Perspectives from Related Arts and*

Disciplines , 86-97. New York: Committee on Research in Dance, 1970.

In a paper delivered at the second Conference on Research in Dance the author discusses the need of ethnic historical study of dance that will yield a history of dance revealing universals and the dynamics of change. Also discusses the theory and method behind "A Comparative Study of Dance as a Constellation of Motor Behaviors among African and United States Negroes," her thesis for Northwestern University. Reports that the results of the study show blacks in the United States having more in common with West Africa in the field of dance and that jazz music evokes a motor response that is interrelated and has its beginnings in Africa.

704. ———. "A Comparative Study of Dance as a Constellation of Motor Behaviors among African and United States Negroes." In *Reflections and Perspectives on Two Anthropological Studies of Dance* , 15-179. New York: Committee on Research in Dance, 1976.

This anthropological study attempts to prove whether or not United States dance behavior includes Africanisms by isolating motor behaviors of Africans and of United States black dancers and then by determining what comparisons are possible between the two dance groups. The author concludes that the motor behaviors do bear close comparison.

705. Kendall, Elizabeth. "New York City Bread and Circus." *Dance Magazine* (Nov. 1974): 79, 81, 83.

A general review of the Delacorte Festival in New York City, 1974. Black dance groups participating were Gus Solomons, Jr., Bottom of the Bucket...But, Sounds in Motion, George Faison's Universal Dance Experience, and the Fred Benjamin Dance Company.

706. ———. "Dancers and Audiences, and Thoughts about Entertainment." *Dance Magazine* (May 1975): 81-83.

Reviews Dianne McIntyre's Sounds in Motion at the Henry Street Playhouse, Mar. 3, 1975.

707. Kennedy, Stetson. "Nañigo in Florida." *Southern Folklore Quarterly* 4 (Sept. 1940): 153-56.

708. Kernodle, Robert. "Audience Takes Percussive Ride." *Carolinian* [Raleigh, N.C.] (Sept. 22, 1981).

Reviews the Chuck Davis Dance Company at the Dana Auditorium.

709. Kerns, Virginia. *Women and the Ancestors.* Urbana, Ill.: University of Illinois Press, 1983.

Discusses Afro-Caribbean women and how they preserve the ceremonial aspects of their culture. The field work was done in a Caribbean town in Belize. Describes dancing as part of their death rites. Also describes John Canoe (wanaragua), pp. 187-88 and mali (dance of placation) pp. 162-63.

710. Kerr, Madeline. *Personality and Conflict in Jamaica.* London: Willmer & Haram, 1963.

Studies culture conflict in Jamaica. Describes folk life including dances, specifically "John Canoe" (pp. 143-44) and "Kumina" (pp. 144-47).

711. "Kid Dance Team." *Ebony* (Oct. 1955): 131-34.

Elia and Michelle Clark.

712. Kidder, Rushworth M. and Maggie Lewis. "Boston Ballet Company Stumbles over the Issue of Race." *Christian Science Monitor* (June 5, 1981).

713. Kimball, Robert. "Tina Yuan Graceful as Gazelle." *New York Post* (Dec. 4, 1976).

Reviews the Alvin Ailey American Theater performing George Faison's "Gazelle."

714. King, Andrea. "Group to Show Black Dance's Spirit." *IDS* [Indiana University] (Apr. 7, 1977).

The Afro-American Dance Company of Indiana University performs.

715. King, Jean. "Carifesta Responsible for Carib. Cultural Revival." *Sunday Graphic* [Georgetown, Guyana] (Oct. 5, 1973).

Lavinia Williams discusses the importance of Carifesta.

716. ———. "The Versatile Lavinia Williams." *The Sunday Argosy* (Apr. 4, 1974).

Interview.

717. Kinney, Esi Sylvia. "Africanisms in Music and Dance of the Americas." In *Black Life and Culture in the United States* edited by Rhoda L. Goldstein, pp. 49-63. New York: Thomas Crowell, 1971.

718. Kisselgoff, Anna. "Eugene James Troupe at Kaufman Hall." *New York Times* (Oct. 21, 1968).

719. ———. "Ron Davis Group in Carnegie Hall." *New York Times* (Jan. 4, 1969).

720. ———. "Dancing and Life Merge in Ron Davis's Classes." *New York Times* (Jan. 7, 1969): 30.

721. ———. "Black Choreographers Go on Display." *New York Times* (Mar. 17, 1969).

In this black choreographers' symposium sponsored by the Harlem Cultural Council and Barnard College, three choreographers—Louis Johnson, Rod Rodgers, and Eleo Pomare—demonstrate their individual style of movement to 136 high school and college students.

722. ———. "Black Expo Presents Dances by Eleo Pomare, Rod Rodgers." *New York Times* (Apr. 26, 1969).

723. ———. "Destiné's Dancers Show Ethnic Grace." *New York Times* (June 15, 1970).

   Reviews Jean-Léon Destiné's company.

724. ———. "Dance" Eleo Pomare Gives Première at ANTA." *New York Times* (Feb. 5, 1971).

   Reviews "Movements" and "Black on Black."

725. ———. "Eleo Pomare Gives Premières at ANTA." *New York Times* (Feb. 25, 1971).

   Reviews a performance at the ANTA Theater, New York City, on Feb. 24, 1971.

726. ———. "Mary Hinkson Powerful in Graham's Medea Role." *New York Times* (May 10, 1973).

   Reviews Hinkson in Martha Graham's "Cave of the Heart."

727. ———. "Ballet: 'Hidden Rites.'" *New York Times* (May 19, 1973).

   Ailey premières new work.

728. ———. "Collins and Primus in Ailey Spotlight." *New York Times* (May 15, 1974).

   Briefly sketches the careers of Janet Collins and Pearl Primus on the occasion of the staging of some of their works by the Ailey company.

729.   ———. "Judith Jamison Offers a Structured Solo." *New York Times* (May 24, 1974).

730.   ———. "Dance: Rod Rodgers Troupe." *New York Times* (Nov. 13, 1976).

731.   ———. "George Faison's 'Gazelle' Danced by Ailey Troupe." *New York Times* (Dec. 5, 1976).

732.   ———. "Estelle Spurlock in Ailey's 'Cry.'" *New York Times* (Dec. 6, 1976).

733.   ———. "A Dance of Time and the Rivers." *New York Times* (Dec. 10, 1976).

Profiles Donald McKayle, his career and recent works.

734.   ———. "Dance: Cincinnatians Display an Eclectic Metier." *New York Times* (Feb. 20, 1977).

Reviews the Cincinnati Ballet performing at Pace University in New York City. This company is a repository of works of Lester Horton.

735.   ———. "Charles Moore Dancers Present Fine Tribute to African Pioneer." *New York Times* (Apr. 3, 1977).

Reviews the Charles Moore Dance Company's tribute to Asadata Dafora at Pace University.

736.   ———. "Dance: By Abbott and Perryman." *New York Times* (July 17, 1977).

Review of performance by Loretta Abbott and Al Perryman.

737.   ———. "Dance: Ailey Opens with 2 Premières." *New York Times* (May 5, 1978).

Reviews the Alvin Ailey American Dance Theater at the City Center, New York City. The works performed: "Passage," "Butterfly" (Rael Lamb), "Gazelle" (Faison), and "Suite Otis."

738. ———. "Harlem Troupe Dances De Lavallade." *New York Times* (Feb. 24, 1979).

Dance Theatre of Harlem dances "Sensemaya."

739. ———. "Pearl Primus Offering Program of Dance Called 'Earth Theater.'" *New York Times* (Mar. 24, 1979).

Reviews a performance at the Theater of the Riverside Church including works of African, Caribbean, and black-American origin such as "Fanga," "La Jablesse," "War Dance," "Dance with Rattles," "Afro-American Scenes," and "Michael Row the Boat Ashore."

740. ———. "Alvin Ailey's Homage to Joyce Trisler." *New York Times* (Dec. 16, 1979).

Reviews Alvin Ailey's choreographic tribute to Trisler entitled "Memoria."

741. ———. "Ballet: 'Allegro Brillante' by the Harlem Company." *New York Times* (Jan. 8, 1981).

Reviews Dance Theatre of Harlem's "Allegro Brillante," which was performed with "Design for Strings," "The Beloved," "Adagietto No. 5," and "Dougla."

742. ———. "Dance: Harlem's One-Act 'Swan Lake.'" *New York Times* (Jan. 15, 1981).

Reviews Dance Theatre of Harlem (also performing "Greening," "The Greatest," "Troy Game").

743.   ———. "Pomare's 'Las Desnamoradas.'" *New York Times* (Feb. 16, 1981).

Reviews the performance of the Eleo Pomare Company at the Symphony Space on Feb. 14, 1981.

744.   ———. "Harlem's 'Frankie and Johnny.'" *New York Times* (Jan. 28, 1982).

Reviews a Dance Theatre of Harlem production.

745.   ———. "Harlem Dance Theatre Steps Out." *New York Times* (Jan. 31, 1982).

Dance Theatre of Harlem takes a new direction with dramatic ballets.

746.   ———. "Limning the Role of the Black Dancer in America." *New York Times* (May 16, 1982): Sect. 2, p. 10.

Reviews "Black Dance in Photographs" exhibit at the Schomburg Center for Research in Black Culture Apr.-May 1982.

747.   ———. "Dance: Black Choreographers' 'Parallels.'" *New York Times* (Oct. 30, 1982).

Reviews a series of concerts by black choreographers held at St. Mark's Church.

748.   Klemesrud, Judy. "A Special with Roots in the Past." *New York Times* (Feb. 28, 1978).

Reviews Ben Vereen and his upcoming television special.

749.   Kmen, Henry A. *Music in New Orleans: The Formative Years 1791-1841.* Baton Rouge: Louisiana State University Press, 1966.

Chapter 2 discusses quadroon balls and Chapter 12, "Negro Music," covers folklore and social dancing, including dancing in Place Congo.

750. Koffman, L.Th. "Vom Urwald in die Bar; die Negertänze Afrikas und Charleston." *Der Tanz* 2, no. 4 (Feb. 1929): 6-9.

751. Kolodin, Irving. "'Black Ritual' Is Danced at Center." *New York Sun* (Jan. 23, 1940).

    Reviews Agnes DeMille's "Black Ritual."

752. ———. "African Dancers Open at Chanin." *New York Sun* (Apr. 9, 1940).

    Reviews "Zunguru" by Asadata Dafora.

753. Krebs, Betty Dietz. "'Black Snow' Realizes Dazzlingly Large Dream." *Dayton Daily News* (Apr. 11, 1976): 13a.

    Reviews a performance of "Black Snow" by the Dayton Contemporary Dance Company.

754. Krehbiel, Henry Edward. *Afro-American Folksongs: A Study in Racial and National Music*. New York: Ungar, 1962.

    One of the early attempts (originally published in 1914) to analyze black-American folk songs. Chapter 9, "Dances of the American Negroes," traces their origins to Africa. Discusses the habanera, calinda, juba, and counjai.

755. Krotje, Carol. "'Mass' Staging Immense Project." *OSU Lantern* (May 14, 1974).

    Profiles Gus Solomons and tells of his work in the staging of Leonard Bernstein's "Mass."

756. Kubik, Gerhard. "Angolan Traits and Black Music, Games and Dances of Brazil." In *Estudos de Antropologia Cultural, no. 10*. Lisbon: Centro de Estudos de Antropologia Cultural, 1979, pp. 7-55.

    A study of African cultural extensions in Brazil, particularly Angolan capoeira.

757. Kuhn, Annette. "Kids." *Village Voice* (Nov, 25, 1969): 22.

Reviews the Afro-American Dance Ensemble at the City Center, N.Y.C. Celebration of the Arts for Children.

758. Kuklin, Susan. *Reaching for Dreams: A Ballet from Rehearsal to Opening Night.* New York: Lothrop, Lee and Shepard Books, 1987.

Alvin Ailey American Dance Theater.

759. Kunkel, Peter and Sara Sue Kennard. *Spout Spring: A Black Community.* New York: Holt, Rinehart and Winston, 1971.

An ethnographic study of a black Arkansas community that describes some dance practices (p. 80).

760. Kurath, Gertrude P. "Stylistic Blends of Afro-American Dance Cults of Catholic Origins." *Papers of the Michigan Academy of Science, Arts and Letters* 48 (1963): 577-84.

Traces the sources of dance in Latin America and the West Indies.

761. [L., R.] R.L. "Dunham Dancers Hit of 'Pop' Concert." *New York Times* (May 7, 1946).

762. [L., S.] S.L. "Negro Dance Theatre of Wilson Williams." *Dance Observer* (Jan. 1946).

763. Laban, Juana de. "What Tomorrow? *Dance Observer* (May 1945): 55-56.

Summarizes the changes in the American dance scene between 1930 and 1945. Martha Graham is quoted as saying that the two traditional sources, Indian and black, had intense psychic significance but were "dangerous and hard to handle in the arts." In the summary Laban observes that one of the real changes by 1945 was the black contribution to dance.

764. La Maute, Michel. "Entretien avec Lavinia Williams." *Le Nouvelliste* (Oct. 18, 1972).

Interviews Lavinia Williams.

765. Lamberterie, R. de. "Notes sur les Bonis de la Guyane Française." *Journal de la Société des Américanistes de Paris* 35 (1947): 123-47.

Gives a history of the Boni, one of the representative Maroon tribes of French Guiana. Mentions their dances briefly (p. 146).

766. Landes, Ruth. *The City of Women.* New York: Macmillan, 1947.

Describes the life of Brazilian blacks as witnessed on an anthropological field trip to Bahia. Describes a men's samba contest (p. 97), a women's samba contest (pp. 107-10). and a capoeira bout (p. 102-07).

767. Lane, Winsome. "Locals Fail to Support Ballet." *Nassau Guardian and Bahamas Observer* (June 26, 1970).

Reviews the Dance Theatre of Harlem.

768. Lanuza, José Luis. *Morenada.* Buenos Aires: Editorial Schapiro S.R.L., 1967.

A history of blacks in Argentina. For material on dances see "Comparsas" (p. 215) and "La Milonga" (including the tango) (p. 223).

769. Larkin, Kathy. "Tall Story." *New York News* (Oct. 19, 1975): 46.

Features Judith Jamison.

770. "The Late 'Pops' Whitman Was on Stage at 3: Starred at 8." *Chicago Defender* (July 22, 1950).

The obituary of Pops of the dance team Pops and Louie.

771. Latham, Jacqueline Quinn Moore. *A Biographical Study of the Lives and Contributions of Two Selected Contemporary Black Male Dancers.* Texas Women's University, 1973.

Ph.D. dissertation studies Alvin Ailey and Arthur Mitchell.

772. Latrobe, Benjamin Henry Boneval. *Impressions Respecting New Orleans; Diary and Sketches 1818-1820.* New York: Columbia University Press, 1951. (Originally published New York, 1905.)

Describes African slave dancing in Congo Square accompanied by sketches of musical instruments used by the dancers (pp. 46-51).

773. "Lavinia Taught Us Discipline." *Sunday Chronicle* [Georgetown, Guyana] (Sept.16, 1973).

A Guyanese dancer gives her opinion of Lavinia William's three-month dance course in Guyana.

774. "Lavinia Williams Acclamée aux U.S.A." *Le Nouvelliste* (Sept. 30, 1959).

775. "Lavinia Williams an Unforgettable Personality." *Daily Chronicle* [Georgetown, Guyana] (Sept. 13, 1973).

776. "Lavinia Williams est Rentrée." *Le Nouvelliste* (Oct. 7, 1969).

Lavinia Williams returns to Haiti after a stay in New York City.

777. Leaf, Earl. *Isles of Rhythm.* New York: A.S. Barnes, 1948.

Leaf's generously photographed book attempts to document the dance of all of the West Indies.

778. Lee, Amy. "Harlem Teen-Agers Dance 'For Real.'" *Christian Science Monitor* (Sept. 12, 1967): 9.

The history of the Ron Davis Dancers.

779. Lee, Betty. *Dancing All the Latest Steps.* New York: Edward J. Clode, Inc., 1926.

Gives instructions and the origins of some of the popular dances of the 1920s. Includes the fox trot as learned by Vernon Castle at "colored night clubs," the black bottom, the ballroom charleston, and St. Louis hop, which may be a version of the lindy hop.

780. Lekis, Lisa. "The Dance as an Expression of Caribbean Folklore." In *The Caribbean: Its Culture* edited by A. Curtis Wilgus, 43-73. Gainesville, Fla.: University of Florida Press, 1955.

States, "Dance expresses, as nothing else can, the temperament, mood, and heritage of the Caribbean." Gives a survey of the dance traditions of the Caribbean and traces their roots. Some of the countries covered are Haiti, Cuba, Trinidad, Puerto Rico, Venezuela, and the Virgin Islands.

781. ———. *Origin and Development of Ethnic Caribbean Dance and Music.* Gainesville, Fla.: University of Florida Press, 1956.

"Attempts to survey the field of Caribbean dance and music and to tie together the racial, historical, and sociological factors that enable us to consider the dance and music...as one cultural unit."

782. ———. *Folk Dances of Latin America.* New York: Scarecrow Press, 1958.

Describes the folk dances of the countries of Latin America and the Caribbean. Includes dances derived from Africa.

783. ———. *Dancing Gods.* New York: Scarecrow Press, 1960.

Describes the dances of the Caribbean Islands in substantial chapters on each major island. Discusses the most common dances, when danced, and what influences played the biggest part (i.e., European or African).

784. Leopoldi, José Savio. *Escola de Samba, Ritual e Sociedade.* Petropolis, Brazil: Editora Vozes Ltda., 1978.

785. Lessa, Barbossa. "Dancing for St. Benedict." *Américas* 8 (1956): 11-16.

Describes a festival in Brazil dating from the days of slavery. Held in Aparecido do Norte, the festival features the congada and mozambique.

786. Lessa, Luis Carlos. "Dancing Gauchos." *Américas* 5, no. 2 (Feb. 1953): 12-19, 46.

Discusses the differences between the dances of the gauchos of Brazil and Uruguay. Demonstrates the African influence on the rhythms of Brazilian gaucho dances.

787. Levinson, André. "The Negro Dance under European Eyes." In *Theatre: Essays on the Arts of the Theatre* edited by Edith J.R. Isaacs, 235-45. Boston: Little, Brown and Company, 1927.

Attempts to interpret black dance as presented by the artists of the Revue Nègre at the Champs Elysées. Author compares classical dance to "primitive" black dance, and black dance to jazz music. Describes the dancing of Josephine Baker and Florence Mills.

788. Lewin, Olive. "Jamaican Folk Music." *Caribbean Quarterly* 14, nos. 1-2 (1968): 49-56.

This survey of types of folk music and dance ceremonies describes the John Canoe, set girl celebrations, and Kumina and Pocomania cermonies.

789. Lewis, Barbara. "Louise Roberts-Clark Champion Director." *New York Amsterdam News* (July 8, 1977): D-5.

Profiles the director of the Clark Center for the Performing Arts in New York City.

790. Lewis, Dan. "Versatile Ben Vereen Stretches His Skill." *New World* (Jan. 1, 1980).

791. Lewis, Julinda. "Von Grona: Pride over Prejudice." *Other Stages* (Dec. 3, 1981).

Describes the original American Negro Ballet Company and Von Grona's attempt to revive it.

792. ———. "A Salute to Black Dance in America: Newark Dance Theatre, Danny Sloan Dance Company, Detroit City Dance Company, National Dance Theatre of Zaire." *Dance Magazine* (Feb. 1982): 36-40.

793. ———. "Fred Benjamin: A Tyrant Matures." *Attitude* (Sept./Oct. 1983): 10-11.

794. ———. "Thelma Hill Performing Arts Center Presents...." *Attitude* 2, no. 6 (Nov. 1983): 24.

Reviews a three-day series in which the Alvin Ailey Repertory Ensemble, Dallas Black Dance Theatre, African Heritage Company (Washington, D.C.), Cleo Parker Dance Ensemble (Denver), and Jubilation! Dance Company (Brooklyn) performed.

795. ———. "Thomas Pinnock Africa-Reggae Dance Theater and the Survival of Africa in the Diaspora." *Attitude* 2, no. 6 (Nov. 1983): 17.

796. Lewis, Maggie. "In Post-Modern Dance, Old Rules Are out—Almost Any Movement Has Its Value." *Christian Science Monitor* (July 29, 1982).

Reviews dance partners Bill T. Jones and Arnie Zane at Harvard Summer Dance Festival.

797. Lewis, Mathew Gregory. *Journal of a West Indian Proprietor, Kept During a Residence in the Island of Jamaica.* London: John Murray, 1834.

Gives an account of planation life on Jamaica during the early nineteenth century. Describes a John Canoe celebration and set girls on New Year's Day (pp. 51-59).

798. "Life Goes to the Starbud's Revue." *Life* (Nov. 6, 1950).

Mary Bruce, well-known Harlem dance teacher, and her group, the Starbuds, perform at Carnegie Hall.

799. Limeira, Eudenise de Albuquerque. *A Comunicação Gestual; Analise Semiotica de Danças Folklóricas Nordestinas.* Rio de Janeiro: Editoria Rio, 1977.

800. "Lindy Hop; A True National Folk Dance Has Been Born in U.S.A." *Life* (Aug. 23, 1943).

801. "Lindy Hoppers Now Kick Heels in First American Negro Ballet." *Herald-News* [Passaic, N.J.] (Dec. 17, 1937).

802. Liscano, Juan. "Hear the People Sing." *Américas* 1, no. 5 (1949): 12-15, 34-45.

Describes black folk dance in Ocumare de Tuy, Venezuela.

803. ———. *Folklore y Cultura.* Caracas: Editorial Avila Grafica, 1950.

Gives some information on dance in the following chapters: "Apuntes Para el Conocimiento de la Población Negra de

Venezuela" and "Las Fiestas del Solsticio de Verano en el Folklore de Venezuela."

804. "Little Daddy." *Ebony* (Jan. 1957): 75-78.

Ben Braddix, managed by Jack Ruby of Dallas, is called another Sammy Davis, Jr.

805. Livingston, Charles. "American Dancer Rediscovered as Dance Teacher down in Haiti." *New Crusader* (Sept. 10, 1960).

Profiles Lavinia Williams.

806. Livingston, D.D. "Taps for Bill Robinson." *Dance Magazine* 24 (Jan. 1950): 13, 46.

Reviews the life and career of Bill Robinson.

807. Lizardo, Fradique. *Danzas y Bailes Folkloricos Dominicanos.* Santo Domingo: Taller, 1974.

808. Lloyd, Margaret. *The Borzoi Book of Modern Dance.* New York: A.A. Knopf, 1949.

Profiles the choreography and careers of Katherine Dunham (pp. 243-53) and Pearl Primus (pp. 265-76) in this history of modern dance.

809. ———. "The Personal Equation: New Ballerina at the Met." *Christian Science Monitor* (Oct. 16, 1951).

Janet Collins.

810. ———. "Designs from Haitian Dance." *Christian Science Monitor* (June 2, 1957).

Reviews a performance including Jean-Léon Destiné, Jeanne Ramon, and Alphonse Cimber in Boston.

811.   Locke, Alain. "Rhythm as a Folk Gift." *Caribe* 7, nos. I & II: 5.

Excerpts from Locke's *Negro and His Music* , first published in 1936.

812.   Lomask, Milton. "Queen of Ballet." *Catholic Digest* (Apr. 1952): 12-18.

Janet Collins.

813.   "London's Sexiest Dancer; Brown Bombshell Fortunia." *Our World* (Apr. 1951): 49-50.

Anita Verna, known as Fortunia, is a night club entertainer in London.

814.   Louis-Jean, Antonio. *La Crise de Possession et la Possession Dramatique* [Montreal]: Les Editions Leméac, 1970.

815.   Louther, William. "Breath and Form." *Dance and Dancers* (Oct. 1977): 28-29, 38.

Talks of movement training for actors and singers.

816.   Lowell, Sondra. "Black Tap Dancing: Sole-to-Soul Feat." *Los Angeles Times* (Apr. 6, 1979): part 4, p. 24.

Reviews "No Maps on My Taps," a documentary film on tap dancing featuring three dancers: Sandman Sims, Bunny Briggs, and Chuck Green.

817.   L'Rue, June. "Want to Learn to Dance?" *Pittsburgh Courier* (Dec. 20, 1952): magazine section.

Describes classes at the Katherine Dunham school in New York City.

818.   Lucas, Bob. "Don Campbell the Wallflower who Invented a Dance...and Became a Star." *Black Stars* (July 1974): 69-74.

Don Campbell invented "lock dancing" and founded the Campbell Lock Dancers featured on various television shows.

819. Lyons, Leonard. "Lyons Den: [Bill Robinson]. *New York Post* (Apr. 4, 1939).

Mrs. Roosevelt invites Robinson to perform with Marian Anderson at Lincoln Memorial.

820. [M., A.D.] A.D.M. "Skilled Dancing in Negro Ballet." *The Bulletin* (Sept. 24, 1957).

The New York Negro Ballet in Scotland.

821. [M., J.] J.M. "The Dance: Negro Art Loses in Originality." *New York Times* (July 8, 1928): Sect. 8, p. 6.

Using Bill Robinson as an example, states that black dance style is a result of "laziness" and that employment of minimal muscular exertion and "Harlemization" will dull good elements in dance.

822. Mackie, Albert. "The Negro Ballet Can Win Friends." *Scottish Daily Express* (Sept. 24, 1957).

The New York Negro Ballet on tour.

823. MacLean y Estenas, Roberto. *Negros en el Mundo Nuevo.* Lima: Editorial P.T.C.M., 1948.

Discusses the slave trade and colonization in the New World. The chapter "Canciones, Poesia, Danza y Musica Negras" (pp. 65-79) defines bamboula, candombe, juba, and religious dancing.

824. Madiana. "The Biguine of the French Antilles." In *Negro Anthology, 1931-1933* edited by Nancy Cunard, 401-02. London: Wishart, 1934.

Discusses the rhythm and patterns of the biguine.

825. "The Madison." *Ebony* (July 1960): 71-74.

826.   "Making Good in Home Town." *Journal and Guide* [Norfolk, Va.] (May 27, 1933).

Discusses the tap dancer Pleasant "Snowball" Crump.

827.   Malmgren, Gert. "Two Brazilian Dances." *Travel in Brazil* 2, no. 3 (1942): 27, 32.

Briefly describes the samba and the frêvo (the dance of the Pernambucano).

828.   "Mambo King; Cuban Negro Creates New Beat that Becomes a Colorful Dance Craze." *Ebony* (Sept. 1951): 45-48.

Profiles Perez Prado, who devised the mambo while in Cuba.

829.   "Mambo Queen." *Hue* (July 1955): 54-57.

Olga Chiaviano of Cuba shows an example of her craft in this photo-story.

830.   "'Mambo' Rocks Cuba." *Our World* (June 1951): 42-45.

831.   "Mambomania." *Newsweek* 44 (Aug. 16, 1954): 54.

832.   Manchester, Phyllis Winifred. "Alvin Ailey Profile." *Dancing Times* (Oct. 1964): 10-11.

Illustrated with photos.

833.   ———. "Meet Donald McKayle." *Dancing Times* (Jan. 1967): 186-87.

834.   Mantle, Burns. "African Opera 50 Stories off the Ground." *New York Daily News* (May 24, 1934).

Reviews Asadata Dafora's "Kykunkor."

835.   "Many Respond to Call for New Ballet Dancers." *New York Amsterdam News* (Sept. 7, 1935).

Eugene Von Grona finds dancers for the American Negro Ballet.

836. Mapp, Edward. *Directory of Blacks in the Performing Arts.* Metuchen, N.J.: Scarecrow Press, 1978.

Alphabetical listing of blacks who have received recognition in the performing arts. Each entry has brief biographical information, professional credits, honors, and career data. The classified index permits access to information by the type of activity, e.g., dancers, 33 of whom are included.

837. Marcelin, Milo. "Danses et Chants Vodou." *Optique* 12 (Feb. 1955): 29-37.

838. Marcus, Elise. "More Low-Down Dancing." *The Dance Magazine* (Jan. 1928): 41.

Buddy Bradley, in photos, shows the sugar foot strut, St. Louis hop, Louisiana mess around, heebie jeebies, Washington Johnny body, mooch, and Virginia essence.

839. Markham, [Dewey] Pigmeat, with Bill Levinson. *Here Come the Judge!* New York: Popular Library, 1969.

The biography of the comic gives a good view of what was a common example of life in show business in tent shows, minstrelsy, and the Theater Owners Booking Association (T.O.B.A.).

840. Marks, Marcia. "Earth Theatre Pearl Primus-Percival Borde Institute." *Dance Magazine* (Aug. 1964): 28.

841. ———. "Dancers of Dancing Parents: Sara Yarborough of Harkness Ballet." *Dance Magazine* (Nov. 1968): 61-63, 98.

Describes the life, education, and career of Lavinia Williams's daughter.

842. ———. "Fred Benjamin Dance Company, Clark Center for the Performing Arts Dec. 1, 1968." *Dance Magazine* (Jan. 1969): 84.

843. ———. "The Alvin Ailey American Dance Theater, Billy Rose Theatre, January 27-February 1, 1969." *Dance Magazine* (Mar. 1969): 92.

844. Marsden, Peter. *An Account of the Island of Jamaica.* Newcastle, England: S. Hodgson, 1788.

Describes a slave Christmas celebration and Saturday night dancing (pp. 33-34).

845. Marsh, Antoinette. "What's Happening." *Black Stars* (Apr. 1977): 22-29.

Fred Berry of the cast of the television series "What's Happening," formerly a member of the Campbell Lock Dancers, is featured on p. 28.

846. Martin, Evelyn. "Self-Expression in Black Dance at St. Marks." *New York Amsterdam News* (Nov. 20, 1982).

Reviews a part of "Parallels," a series of performances of the works of eight black choreographers. Choreographers featured in this part: Rrata Christine Jones, Blondell Cummings, and Ishmael Houston Jones.

847. Martin, John. "The Dance: The Art of the Negro." *New York Times* (July 7, 1929).

Reviews Charles H. Williams' book *Cotton Needs Pickin'* .

848. ———. "Dance Recital Given by Negro Artists." *New York Times* (Apr. 30, 1931).

Reviews Edna Guy and Hemsley Winfield in a performance at the Theatre in the Clouds, Chanin Building, New York City.

849.   ——. "Artistic Endeavor of Negro Dance Wins Commendation." *St. Louis Argus* (Feb. 26, 1932).

Reprinted review of the New Negro Art Theater dance group's debut at the Roxy in New York City.

850.   ——. "The Dance: Negro Art." *New York Times* (Nov. 7, 1937).

Profiles Eugene Von Grona and the American Negro Ballet Company.

851.   ——. "Negro Ballet Has Debut in Harlem." *New York Times* (Nov. 22, 1937).

Reviews debut of the American Negro Ballet Company.

852.   ——. "The Dance: Zunguru." *New York Times* (Aug. 7, 1938).

Reviews the performance of Asadata Dafora's second dance drama.

853.   ——. "DeMille Ballet Seen as Novelty." *New York Times* (Jan. 23, 1940).

Ballet Theater dances Agnes DeMille's "Black Ritual."

854.   ——. "Negro Dance Art Shown in Recital." *New York Times* (Feb. 19, 1940).

Reviews the debut of Katherine Dunham and her group.

855.   ——. "The Dance: A Negro Art." *New York Times* (Feb. 25, 1940).

Discusses Katherine Dunham's debut and her accomplishments.

856. ———. "Dance-Opera Given by Dafora Group." *New York Times* (Mar. 21, 1940).

Reviews Mar. 20, 1940 performance of "Zunguru" at the Cherry Lane Theatre.

857. ———. "The Dance: Elysian Jazz." *New York Times* (Nov. 10, 1940).

Reviews Katherine Dunham in "Cabin in the Sky."

858. ———. "The Dance: Broadway." *New York Times* (Jan. 14, 1951).

Review of Hanya Holm's "Out of this World," featuring Janet Collins.

859. ———. "The Dance: Opera." *New York Times* (Oct. 21, 1956).

On the coming of Geoffrey Holder as solo dancer to the Metropolitan Opera.

860. ———. "Dance: Nice Work." *New York Times* (Nov. 18, 1956).

Reviews Geoffrey Holder in "Aida."

861. ———. "Dance: Good Job." *New York Times* (Dec. 6, 1959).

"Talley Beatty creates an original work in 'The Road of Phoebe Snow.'"

862. ———. "The Dance: In Liberia." *New York Times* (July 31, 1960).

Pearl Primus directs the first African Performing Arts Center in Monrovia.

863. Martin, John Joseph. *The Dance; The Story of the Dance Told in Pictures and Text.* New York: Tudor Publishing, 1947.

"Negro Dance" (pp. 145-47) gives an optimistic look at the development of black dance companies such as the Pearl Primus Company and Katherine Dunham Dance Company.

864. Martin, K.K. "America's First African Dance Theater." *Caribe* 7, nos. I & II: 6-10.

The career of Asadata Dafora and his company. Reprinted from *ODU* (Jan. 1975).

865. Martin, Kathi L. "Dancin' Machine." *Pacific Sun* [Mill Valley, Calif.] (July 1, 1982).

David Alonzo Jones, Calif. dancer of Afro-Haitian-jazz synthesis.

866. "Mary Bruce Dancers Set for Recital." *New York Amsterdam News* (Dec. 4, 1943).

Famous Harlem dance teacher plans her annual revue starring 200 pupils at the Renaissance Ball Room.

867. Maschal, Richard. "Chuck Davis Dance Group." *Charlotte Observer* (Jan. 16, 1980).

868. Maskey, Jacqueline. "Donald McKayle and Company. Hunter College Assembly Hall, March 6, 1964." *Dance Magazine* (Apr. 1964): 73.

869. ———. "Black Rhythms, Circle in the Square, New York." *Dance Magazine* (July 1965): 32, 61.

Pearl Primus and her company in performance in Spring 1965.

870. ———. "Eleo Pomare Dance Company. 92nd Street 'Y' Oct. 16, 1966." *Dance Magazine* (Dec. 1966): 72.

871. ———. "Ron Davis Dancers at Kaufman Hall." *New York Times* (May 27, 1968).

872.   Mason, Nancy. "New York Dance Festival Delacorte Theater, Central Park September 13, 14, 1971." *Dance Magazine* (Nov. 1971): 88-89.

Reviews the George Faison Universal Dance Experience.

873.   ———. "The Solomons Company." *Dance Magazine* (Dec. 1972).

Reviews a performance of Gus Solomons and his company at the Cubiculo, New York City.

874.   "Matt Turney—Dancer." *Crisis* (Apr. 1958): 212-15.

875.   Matthews, Bob. "The Madison." *Afro-American* (Mar. 26, 1960): 1, magazine section.

The over-21 group invents a new dance that becomes a craze.

876.   Matthews, Brander. "The Rise and Fall of Negro Minstrelsy." *Scribner's Magazine* (June 1915): 754-59.

877.   Matthews, Ralph. "Looking at the Stars." *Afro-American* (Nov. 12, 1932).

Relates ancedotes about Bill Robinson.

878.   Maurice, Dick. "Ben Vereen's Christian Verities." *News World* (July 17, 1980).

879.   Maximovna, Elena. "Negro Dance on the Scene." *Dance Magazine* (Dec. 1942): 15, 24.

Discusses the Wilson Williams Negro Dance Company.

880.   Maychick, Diana. "Vereen Traces His Success to 'Roots.'" *New York Post* (Dec. 3, 1982).

881. Maynard, Olga. "Apparitions in Dance." *Dance Magazine* 37 (Oct. 1963): 32-35, 58-59.

Compares candomble and candomble de caboclo (sacred dances of the Amazonian interior). In a note on p. 58 candomble of Bahia is compared to salaca of northern Trinidad showing that Xangu of Bahia is Shango of Trinidad with common roots in the Yoruba of Africa.

882. ———. "Arthur Mitchell and the Dance Theatre of Harlem." *Dance Magazine* (Mar. 1970): 52-64.

883. ———. "Judith Jamison 'More than a Choreographic Instrument.'" *Dance Magazine* (Oct. 1972): 24-29.

884. ———. "Books in Review: Black Dance (in the United States from 1619 to 1970) by Lynne Fauley Emery." *Dance Magazine* (Apr. 1973): 104, 107.

885. ———. "Gary Chryst." *Dance Magazine* 48 (Nov. 1974): 54-57.

886. ———. "Dance Theatre of Harlem: Arthur Mitchell's Dark and Brilliant Splendor." *Dance Magazine* (May 1975): 51-66.

887. ———. *Judith Jamison, Aspects of a Dancer.* Garden City, N.Y.: Doubleday, 1982.

888. McBurnie, Beryl. *Outlines of the Dance of Trinidad.* Port-of-Spain: Guardian Commercial Printery, n.d.

Gives directions for dancing the limbo, shango, bongo, bélé, gran'bélé, and the nation in this brief history of the dances of Trinidad.

889. ———. "The Belaire." *Shell Trinidad* 2 (Mar. 1958): 12-15.

Describes in detail the belaire, also known as bélé, one of the most popular folk dances of Trinidad.

890.   ———. "West Indian Dance." In *The Artist in West Indian Society, A Symposium* edited by Erroll Hill, pp. 51-54. St. Augustine, Trinidad: Department of Extra-Mural Studies, University of the West Indies, 1963.

Summary of a lecture-demonstration and a brief history of the Trinidadian dance stressing the cultural influences on Trinidadian dance.

891.   ———. "The Little Carib and the West Indian Dance." *Caribbean Quarterly* 14, nos. 1 & 2 (1968): 136-39.

The history of the Little Carib Theatre, a group performing traditional Trinidadian dances. Beryl McBurnie was the group's founder.

892.   McDonagh, Don. "Dances of Africa Given on a Program by Pearl Primus." *New York Times* (July 27, 1967).

893.   ———. "Miss De Lavallade Dances Spirituals at Park Festival." *New York Times* (Sept. 5, 1967).

894.   ———. "Dance and Song Pay Tribute to Dr. King." *New York Times* (June 10, 1968).

Reviews Carmen De Lavallade.

895.   ———. "City Center's Fare Seeks to Entertain the Young and Old." *New York Times* (Nov. 17, 1969).

Reviews a performance of the Afro-American Dance Ensemble at the City Center, New York City, for the festival "Celebration of the Arts for Children."

896.   ———. *The Rise and Fall and Rise of Modern Dance*. New York: Outbridge and Dienstfrey, 1970.

Explains modern dance through a series of individual profiles of major modern dance choreographers. Gus Solomons is the only black choreographer covered.

897. ———. "Beatty Dance Pays a Tribute to King." *New York Times* (Sept. 6, 1970).

   Reviews Talley Beatty's "Bring My Servant Home."

898. ———. "Two Faison Dances, 'Slaves' and 'Poppy' Deliver Messages." *New York Times* (May 26, 1971).

899. ———. "African Influence Marks [Chuck] Davis Dance." *New York Times* (Jan. 13, 1974).

900. ———. "Three Revivals Close Exuberant Season by Ailey Dancers." *New York Times* (June 4, 1974).

   The revivals were Katherine Dunham's "Choros," and "Fanga" and "the Wedding" by Pearl Primus.

901. ———. "A Warm Conclusion in M'Intyre Dance." *New York Times* (Apr. 5, 1975).

   Reviews Sounds in Motion at the Henry Street Settlement.

902. ———. "Dancemobile in Series on Harlem Stage." *New York Times* (Jan. 31, 1976).

   Reviews the opening of a series at Harlem Performance Center.

903. ———. "Anger in Verse and Drama." *New York Times* (Dec. 8, 1976).

   The Ailey company in John Park's "You and the Ladies."

904. ———. Ailey Shines in 'Hobo Sapiens.'" *New York Times* (Dec. 9, 1976).

905. ———. "Chuck Davis Changes Style in Afro Dance." *New York Times* (Feb. 26, 1977).

906. ——. "Dance: Rudy Perez 'Coverage II.'" *New York Times* (May 7, 1977).

Reviews a performance by Clive Thompson and the Ailey company.

907. ——. "A New Work by Miss McIntyre, 'Journey to Forever,' a Bad Trip." *New York Times* (May 22, 1977).

908. ——. "Thelma 'Mother' Hill Dies at 53; Noted Teacher of Black Dancers." *New York Times* (Nov. 23, 1977).

909. McHarry, Charles "Pals to Give Bojangles Big Broadway Send Off." *New York News* (Nov. 27, 1949).

910. ——. "One Million Bid Bill Robinson Last 'So Long.'" *New York News* (Nov. 29, 1949).

911. ——. "Real Voodooists Shun that Old Black Magic." *New York News* (May 6, 1957).

Geoffrey Holder expounds on voodoo and how he adapts its rites to the stage.

912. McMahon, John R. "Unspeakable Jazz Must Go! It Is Worse than Saloon and Scarlet Vice, Testify Professional Dance Experts." *Ladies Home Journal* 38 (Dec. 1921): 34, 115-16.

Describes the efforts of the American National Association of Masters of Dancing to reform jazz dancing and allow room for "respectable dancing."

913. McNamara, Rosalind. "Music in the Caribbean," Parts 1 and 2. *Caribbean* 14, nos. 3 & 4 (1960): 45-50; 69-70, 84-85, 100.

Analyzes how the combination of surviving African musical traditions and outside influences contributed to a distinct folk song and dance style in each of the Caribbean islands.

914. McNeil, Albert J. "Sharps and Flats." *California Eagle* (May 19, 1949).

Reviews the First Negro Classic Ballet, later known as the Hollywood Negro Ballet.

915. Mellow, James R. "The Toast of Paris." *New York Times Book Review* (Mar. 29, 1981), 13, 26.

Reviews *Naked at the Feast* by Lynn Haney, a biography of Josephine Baker.

916. Mennesson-Rigaud, Odette. "Vodu Haitien. Quelques Notes sur les Reminiscences Africaines." In *Les Afro-Americains* , 235-44. Institute Française d'Afrique Noire Memoir no. 27. Dakar, 1953.

On voodoo rites and ritual dances.

917. Merizalde del Carmen, P. Bernardo. *Estudio de la Costa Colombiana del Pacífico.* Bogotá: Impr. del Estado Mayor General, 1921.

A study of the Pacific lowlands of Colombia ca. 1900 with a description of the dances of "los negros" on pp. 153-54.

918. Merwin, Bruce W. "A Voodoo Drum from Hayti." *University of Pennsylvania Museum Journal* 8 (1917): 123-25.

An account of voodoo and obeah beliefs. There is some description of the ceremonies and dances.

919. Meryman, Richard. *Louis Armstrong—a Self Portrait.* Millerton, N.Y.: Eakins, 1971.

Armstrong speaks of his life and career and discusses wakes, funeral parades, and dancing in the New Orleans of the early 1900s.

920. Mesmer, Marie. "Ballet Review: Hollywood Negro Ballet." *Daily News* [Los Angeles] (July 12, 1952).

Reviews fourth season of the company.

921. Métraux, Alfred. "La Culte Vodou en Haiti." *La Revue de Paris* 60, no. 8 (1953): 119-29.

922. ———. *Haiti: Black Peasants and Voodoo.* New York: Universe Books, 1960. Translated from *Haiti: La Terre des Hommes et les Dieux.*

Includes a photo essay on dance.

923. Micklin, Bob. "Exploring the Black Experience through Dance." *Newsday* (Mar. 30, 1973): 4A.

A college Afro-American cultural festival brings awareness of black culture to American dance.

924. ———. "Dance Review: Dance Theatre of Harlem." *Newsday* (Feb. 21, 1979).

Dance Theatre of Harlem performs "Agon," "Bugaku," and "Four Temperaments."

925. Millar, Robins. "Intoxicating...this 'Tom-Tom' Ballet." *Scottish Daily Express* (Sept. 10, 1957).

Reviews the New York Negro Ballet in Glasgow.

926. Millstein, Gilbert. "Harlem Stompers." *New York World-Telegram Week-End Magazine* (Jan. 23, 1937): 3.

Describes typical shows at the Apollo with pictures of Alice Whitman of the Whitman Sisters company.

927. ———. "Man of Many Muses." *New York Times Magazine* (Jan. 20, 1957): 46.

Profiles Geoffrey Holder and Carmen De Lavallade.

928. "Miracle on a Stump." *Our World* (Dec. 1950): 55-57.

Peg Leg Bates.

929. "Miss Dunham Trains Dancers for New Film." *Ebony* (Oct. 1958): 121-22, 124.

Katherine Dunham choreographs the film "Green Mansions."

930. Mitchell, Bruce. "Heavy Fantastic." *Magazine of the Year* (Aug. 1947).

Photo story shows jitterbugging at the Savoy.

931. "Moke and Poke Quit Lenox Av. Sidewalk for Broadway Stage." *New York Post* (May 29, 1942).

Nat Nazzaro signs the dance team Moke and Poke in this photo story.

932. Monahan, James. "Harlem at the Wells." *Dancing Times* (Oct. 1976): 20-21.

Analyzes the Dance Theatre of Harlem's second visit to the Sadler's Wells in London.

933. Monplaisir, Emma. *La Martinique et Ses Danses.* Fort de France, Martinique: Imp. Bezaudin, 1962.

934. Monroe, Al. "Billy McClain, Friend of Kings, Retires." *Chicago Defender* (Mar. 18, 1933).

Gives the life and career of showman who supposedly started the cakewalk while appearing in "The South before the War."

935.   Moore, Joseph G. "Religious Syncretism in Jamaica." *Practical Anthropology* 12, no. 2 (Mar.-Apr. 1965): 63-70.

Describes religious syncretism in the Revival, Zionist, and Pocomania Cults. Describes rituals, particularly the Cumina ritual dances.

936.   Moore, Lillian. "Moreau de Saint-Méry and 'Danse.'" *Dance Index* 5, no. 10 (Oct. 1946): 232-59.

Excerpts and comments on *Danse* , the first book on the subject issued in the United States; it deals with traditional dancing on Haiti, then called Santo Domingo.

937.   ———. "'Les Sylphides' Is Dance at the Theatre-in-the-Park." *New York Herald Tribune* (Aug. 15, 1959).

Reviews the Ballet Russe de Monte Carlo and mentions Raven Wilkinson.

938.   ———. "Donald McKayles's 'Black New World' at YM-YWHA, New York, Feb. 8, 1967." *Dance News* (Mar. 1967): 10.

939.   Moore, William. "The Other Dance: A Statement about the A.B.C." *Dance Scope* 3, no. 2 (Spring 1967): 26-29.

States the purpose of the Association of Black Choreographers.

940.   ———. "How to Be a Good Critic of Dance." *The Feet* (June 1973): 21.

941.   ———. "Capoeira in Rio." *Times of Brazil* (Oct. 7, 1973).

942.   ———. "Dance in Brazil! An Overall Look." *Times of Brazil* (Oct. 14, 1973).

943.   ———. "Road of Black Dance and Those who Paved the Way." *Contact* (Spring 1974): 28-31.

944. ———. "Reflections and Perceptions on Black Dance." *The Western Journal of Black Studies* 1, no. 4 (Dec. 1977): 276-77.

Holds the view that black dance is just beginning and that white critics have been destructive to its new creativeness. Feels the turning point will come when communication between artists and the public improves.

945. ———. "Dancer Walter Nicks: A Master of Movement." *New York Amsterdam News* (Dec. 1, 1979): 33.

Reviews the Walter Nicks Dance Theatre performing at the Riverside Theater.

946. Morazan, Ronald R. "'Quadroon' Balls in the Spanish Period." *Louisiana History* 14, no. 3 (Summer 1973): 310-15.

Reviews the city documents of New Orleans that first granted permission for blacks to have public dance halls.

947. "More than Enough at N.Y. City Ballet." *Dance and Dancers* (Mar. 1961): 29-30.

Reviews Balanchine's "Modern Jazz: Variants" with Arthur Mitchell and John Jones dancing.

948. Moreau de Saint-Méry, Médéric Louis Élie. *Dance; An Article Drawn from the Work of M.L.E. Moreau de St.-Méry Entitled: Repertory of Colonial Information Compiled Alphabetically (1796).* Translated by Lily and Baird Hastings. New York: Dance Horizons, 1976.

This translation of a book believed to be the first published book on dance in the United States gives Moreau de St.-Méry's ideas on dance. To vary his observations he uses examples based on studies of the New World. Describes Creole balls in Santo Domingo, the chica, Creole dances of Curaçao, freedman dances, and slave dances like the Kalenda, the Vaudoux, and Dance of Don Pedro.

949. ———. *Danse*. Philadelphia: published by the author, 1976. Another edition published in Parma by Bodoni, 1803.

950. ———. "Danses des Noirs d'Amérique au XVIIIe Siècle." In *Beauté de la Danse* edited by Gilberte Cournand, 39-51. Paris: Gautier-Langereau, [1977].

951. Morgan, Clyde. "Art Had a Power Then." *Dance Scope* 3, no. 2 (Spring 1967): 23-25.

Morgan reminisces about his time as a dancer at the Karamu Playhouse.

952. Morrison, "Hen." "Charleston Dates Way Back. Is It Here to Stay?" *Chicago Bee* (July 10, 1926).

953. Morton, Virgil L. *The Teaching of Popular Dance*. Illustrated by Hilda Sachs. New York: J.L. Pratt, 1966.

Aids instructors of popular dancing at high school and college levels, but could be used for any beginner. Includes instructions for cha cha, Argentine tango, swing (lindy, shag, jitterbug), samba, fox trot, and American rumba. Each chapter includes a brief essay on dance origins.

954. Moss, Allyn. "Who is Geoffrey Holder?" *Dance Magazine* (Aug. 1958): 36-41.

955. "Mourn Passing of Ella Gordon." *New York Age* (Nov. 21, 1936).

Obituary of a well-known Harlem dance teacher.

956. "Movie Dance Director; Marie Bryant Teaches Dancing Routines to Hollywood Stars." *Ebony* (Apr. 1950): 22-26.

957. Mueller, John. *Dance Film Directory; An Annotated and Evaluative Guide to Film on Ballet and Modern Dance*. University of Rochester: Princeton Books Company, 1979.

A directory of 16mm. dance films available through distributors with notes and evaluative material, including some black dancers and choreographers.

958. Mujica Laínez, Roberto. "The Tango Story." *Américas* 7, no. 4 (Apr. 1955): 13.

959. "Multi-racial Ballet of the 20th Century Company Here." *New York Amsterdam News* (Oct. 21, 1972): D-1.

960. Murphy, Agnes. "At Home with...Carmen De Lavallade." *New York Post* (Dec. 2, 1967).

961. Murphy, Frederick Douglas. "Debbie Allen: A View from Within the Heart of an Actress." *Black Stars* (Apr. 1979): 6-9.

962. Murphy, Richard W. "On Stage: Carmen De Lavallade." *Horizon* (May 1963): 48-49.

963. "Myrna White Scores Dance Success." *Ebony* (Apr. 1963): 59-64.

White was the first black dancer to integrate the Ed Sullivan Show's permanent dance troupe.

964. Nash, Joe. "Dancing Many Drums." *National Scene Magazine Supplement* (Sept.-Oct. 1976): 1-3, 8-12.

965. "Nashville Revels in Carnival Bash." *States-Item* [New Orleans] (Feb. 11, 1977).

Reviews "Fat Tuesday (and All that Jazz)," performed by the Arthur Hall Afro-American Dance Ensemble in Nashville.

966. *National Dance Theatre Company of Jamaica.* N.p.: Desnoes and Geddes, Ltd., 1966.

Pictorial presentation of the company.

967. "Negro Ballet." *Newcastle Journal* (Sept. 16, 1957).

Reviews the New York Negro Ballet in Newcastle, England.

968. "Negro Teaches Rockette Folk Dancing." *Hue* (Aug. 1958): 16-18.

Lavinia Williams teaches Haitian-born Norma Chauvet the art of Haitian dance.

969. "Negroes in Ballet." *Dance and Dancers* (Oct. 1957): 9.

Discusses the New York Negro Ballet and its attempt to present classical dance with a black heritage theme. Written on the occasion of the company's English tour.

970. "Negroes Make All Ballet Exotic." *Journal and North Mail* (Sept. 17, 1957).

Reviews the New York Negro Ballet in Newcastle, England.

971. "Negro's Contribution to American Art." *Literary Digest* 55, no. 16 (Oct. 20, 1917): 26-27.

Discusses the folkloric importance of spirituals, slave songs, Uncle Remus stories, the clog and the jug, ragtime and blues.

972. Nettel, Reginald. "Historical Introduction to 'La Calinda.'" *Music and Letters* 27, no. 1 (Jan. 1946): 59-62.

973. Nettl, Paul. "Traces of the Negroid in the 'Mauresque' of the Sixteenth and Seventeenth Centuries." *Phylon* 5, no. 2 (1944): 105-13.

974. Nettleford, Rex. "Jamaica." *Dance and Dancers* (Nov. 1965): 20-23.

Interview with the director of the Jamaica National Dance Theatre.

975. ———. "The Dance as an Art Form—Its Place in the West Indies." *Caribbean Quarterly* 14, no. 1-2 (1968): 127-35.

Discusses the art of dance and the transformation of the various folk elements into a theatrical setting reflecting a truly national (Jamaican) art dance.

976. ———. "Pocomania in Dance-Theatre." *Jamaica Journal* 3, no. 2 (1969): 21-24.

Discusses the problem of adapting the dances of Pocomania to the stage.

977. ———. *Roots and Rhythms: Jamaica's National Dance Theatre.* New York: Hill and Wang, 1969.

Gives the roots, repertoire, objectives, training of and contributors to the Jamaica National Dance Theatre Company. Includes many photographs.

978. "New Dance Craze Booming in Miami, Florida." *Pittsburgh Courier* (May 26, 1962): 19.

Discusses the chicken scratch.

979. "New Kick in Brazil." *Time* 99 (May 1, 1972): 84.

Gives the origins and steps of capoeira in Brazil.

980. "New Queen of Ballet." *Jet* (May 14, 1953): 60-61.

Carmen De Lavallade.

981. "A New Vitality." *Charlotte Metrolina Magazine* 4, no. 3 (Jan./Feb. 1972).

982. "New York's 'Craziest' Family." *Sepia* (July 1960): 14-18.

Life with Geoffrey Holder and Carmen De Lavallade.

983. "Newest Ballet Star." *Ebony* (Nov. 1954): 36-40.

Profiles Jamie Bower, the only United States ballerina in the Ballets de Paris of Roland Petit.

984. Newman, Thelma. "Here's Proof: Nothing Else Is Like Ailey." *The Post* [West Palm Beach, Fla.] (Apr. 9, 1981): B7.

Reviews the Alvin Ailey American Dance Theater performing "Night Creatures," "Rainbow 'Round My Shoulder," and "Revelations" at the West Palm Beach Auditorium.

985. Newton, Edmund. "Dance Theatre of Harlem Holds Gala Homecoming." *New York Post* (Nov. 14, 1973).

Fourth anniversary benefit performance.

986. "Nicholas Brothers Biggest Split; Harold, Fayard are 7000 Apart." *Ebony* (May 1960): 77-80.

The Nicholas Brothers act splits up when Fayard returns to the United States while Harold stays in Paris.

987. "Nicholas Brothers: Our Three Gravy Years in Europe." *Our World* (Jan. 1952): 24-27.

988. "Nicholas Brothers Steppin' High with 50 Years of Success." *Jet* (June 25, 1981): 56-57.

Profiles the career of the dance team.

989. Nissen, Johann Peter. *Reminiscences of a 46 Years' Residence in the Island of St. Thomas in the West Indies*. Nazareth, Pa.: Senseman, 1838.

Describes slave dancing and a New Year's celebration.

990. "No Maps on My Taps." *Variety* (Mar. 21, 1979).

Reviews the film featuring Sandman Sims, Bunny Briggs, and Chuck Green.

991. "No. 1 Tap Dancer." *Life* (Dec. 6, 1943).

Features Buck and Bubbles and Bill Bailey.

992. Northrup, Solomon. *Twelve Years a Slave.* Cincinnati: Henry W. Derby, 1853.

Autobiography of an ex-slave musician describes dance and Christmas festivals.

993. Norton, Mildred. [First Negro Classic Ballet.] *Daily News* [Los Angeles] (Sept. 15, 1951).

Later known as the Hollywood Negro Ballet.

994. Nuchtern, Jean. "Back to Africa." *Soho Weekly News* (Mar. 29, 1979).

Review of the Pearl Primus-Percival Borde Dance Company performing "Earth Theater" at the Theater of the Riverside Church in New York City.

995. O'Connor, John. "TV: Ben Vereen Stars in Special on ABC." *New York Times* (Mar. 2, 1978).

996. "The Odds Too Long—Black Dancers and the British Ballet." *Dance and Dancers* (Sept. 1984): 3.

A letter to the editor discusses the lack of opportunity in Great Britain for black dancers.

997. "O'Dwyer to Speak at Bill Robinson Rites." *New York Times* (Nov. 27, 1949).

998. O'Gara, Sheila. *Tap It.* New York: A.S. Barnes and Company, 1937.

Gives basic tap steps and a collection of tap dances and original music.

999. O'Hara, Delia. "A Weird, Wild Dance with a Long History." *Christian Science Monitor* (Oct. 18, 1977).

Gives a brief history of John Canoe in Jamaica.

1000. Ohl, Dorothea Duryea. "Notes on the Cha-Cha, the Mambo and the Merengue." *Dance Magazine* 30 (Mar. 1956): 42-44.

1001. ———. "Calypso Bandwagon." *Dance Magazine* (Mar. 1957): 53-54.

Gives the steps of Geoffrey Holder's calypso.

1002. ———. "Dance Cruise to Haiti." *Dance Magazine* (Sept. 1957): 60-61.

Ohl visits Haiti and discovers Ibo, a meringue variation.

1003. ———. "Dance Cruise II." *Dance Magazine* (Oct. 1957): 56.

Ohl travels to Panama and Haiti to learn native and social dances.

1004. O'Keefe, Margaret. "Eye of the Crocodile." *Attitude* 1, no. 3 (July 1982): 3, 6.

Reviews a collaborative piece by Dianne McIntyre's Sounds in Motion and pianist Cecil Taylor.

1005. Oliveira, Valdemar de. "O Frêvo e o Passo, de Pernambuco." *Boletin Latino American de Musica* 6 (Apr. 1946): 157-92.

1006. Olga. "Jazz Dancing—and Nothing Else But!" *PM* (Feb. 21, 1943).

Asadata Dafora and Mura Dehn teach jazz dancing at the Academy of Jazz dance studio.

1007. "On the Gypsy Circuit: Lester Wilson." *Dance Magazine* (Feb. 1966): 16.

Profiles the choreographer-dancer.

1008. "One-legged, One-armed Dancer; Crip Heard Performs Amazing Act without Crutch, Does Routines from Lindy to Mambo." *Ebony* (Nov. 1951): 47-50.

1009. "1935 Dance Team: It's Shirley Temple and Bill Robinson." *New York Herald Tribune* (Mar. 3, 1935).

Bill Robinson creates a new stair dance to include Shirley Temple for the movie "The Little Colonel."

1010. Orme, Frederic L. "The Negro in the Dance as Katherine Dunham Sees Him." *The American Dancer* 11 (Mar. 1938): 10, 46.

1011. Ortiz Fernandez, Fernando. *Los Bailes y el Teatro de los Negros en el Folklore de Cuba.* Habana: Publicaciones del Ministerio de Educacion, 1951.

1012. Osman, Raschid. "We Can Make a Superb Stage Show Out of Cumfa." *Sunday Graphic* [Georgetown, Guyana] (June 17, 1973).

Lavinia Williams discusses the ritual cumfa and the possibilities of developing a Guyanese National Dance Institute.

1013. Ottley, Carlton, Robert. *Tobago: Robinson Crusoe's Island in the West Indies.* Port-of-Spain, Trinidad: P.N.M. Publishing Co., 1969.

Describes a wedding reel, held on the eve of a wedding, in which the dancers are possessed by the spirits of the groom's dead relatives (pp. 76-79).

1014. "Out of this World; West Coast's Gift to Broadway is Dancer Janet Collins." *Our World* (June 1951): 54-55.

1015.   [P., M.] M.P. "Asadata Dafora and Group." *Dance Observer*
(Dec. 1947): 114-15.

1016.   [P., P.] P.P. "National Ballet Aantrekkelijke Première van De
Vuurvogel." *De Volkskrant* (Dec. 12, 1967).

Mentions Raven Wilkinson.

1017.   [P., S.] S.P. "Geoffrey Holder: Dancer who Paints." *New York
Times* (Feb. 4, 1955).

Holder exhibits his paintings at the Barone Gallery.

1018.   Paine, Lewis W. *Six Years in a Georgia Prison.*   New York:
Printed for the author, 1851.

A white man relates his life in the South and his time in prison
for helping a slave escape. Chapter 16 describes amusements: a
log rolling celebration with dancing, patting juba, a shucking frolic,
and a Christmas celebration.

1019.   Panassié, Hugues. "Le Jazz et la Danse." *Formes et Couleurs* 10,
no. 4 (1948): 96-104.

1020.   Pandolfi, Joyce Verhalen. "Tale of Two Cities...Boston and Los
Angeles." *Dance Herald* 1, no. 1 (1975): 3.

Reports on the Elma Lewis School of Boston and the Inner
City Center of Los Angeles.

1021.   "Paris Ballet Star." *Ebony* (Dec. 1967): 67-68, 70, 72, 74.

Profiles American-born Norman de Joie who made his career in
Paris with Les Ballets Modernes de Paris. He began dancing as a
student with Lester Horton and also studied with Syvilla Fort and
Margaret Craske.

1022.   Parker, Jerry. "Ben Vereen, White House Draftee." *Newsday*
(Mar. 19, 1976).

Ben Vereen performs for President Ford at the White House.

1023. Parson, Thomas E. *How to Dance.* Revised ed. New York: Barnes and Noble, 1965.

Gives the steps to the fox trot, rumba, tango, mambo, samba, merengue, cha cha, twist, and American swing (variations on the lindy).

1024. Pastore, Louise. "Movements Black: Dance Repertory Theatre, Inc. The Cubiculo October 27, 1970." *Dance Magazine* (Jan. 1971): 71.

Review.

1025. ———. "Eleo Pomare Dance Company, ANTA Theater, N.Y.C. February 4-6, 1971." *Dance Magazine* (Apr. 1971): 96.

1026. Patrick, Michelle A. "Dance Theatre of Harlem." *Dawn Magazine* (Oct. 1982): 20.

1027. Patterson, Orlando. *The Sociology of Slavery: An Analysis of the Origins, Development, and Structure of Negro Slave Society in Jamaica.* Rutherford, N.J.: Fairleigh Dickinson University Press, 1967.

Attempts to explain the structure of Jamaican slave society. Discusses dancing in Chapter 8, "Social Institutions of the Slaves." The possible African origins of John Canoe are also discussed.

1028. Patton, Bernice. "Bill Robinson who Learned to Dance on Streets Teaches Hollywood to Tap." *Chicago Defender* (Feb. 2, 1935).

1029. ———. "New York's 'Mayor of Harlem' Born in Virginia, Began Dancing for a Living at Early Age of Seven." *Journal and Guide* [Norfolk, Va.] (Feb. 22, 1936).

Bill Robinson.

1030. "Paul Grey of Downtown Ballet Company Performs 'Satchmo' Tribute." *New York Amsterdam News* (Dec. 23, 1972): D-1.

1031. Pavie, Théodore. *Souvenirs Atlantiques* , 2 vols. Paris: Roret, Rue Hautefeuille-Renouard-Hector Bossange, Arthur-Bertrand-Treuttel et Wurtz, 1833.

Describes dancing and music in the South (vol. 2, pp. 319-20).

1032. "Pavlova Never Danced Like This." *Life* (Sept. 15, 1941).

Photo story on the Harvest Moon ball at the Savoy Ballroom.

1033. "Pearl Primus; Foremost Dancer to Unveil New Exciting Work Based on Long Study of African People." *Ebony* (Jan. 1951): 54-58.

1034. Pearlman, Joseph. "Harlemites Foresake Torrid 'Swing' Dances for the Modern Ballet Steps." *Times Herald* (Dec. 12, 1937).

Reviews the debut of the American Negro Ballet.

1035. "Pearl's Prodigy; Pearl Primus Unveils New Dancing Star, Percival Borde." *Ebony* (Mar. 1959): 47-50.

1036. "'Peckin' Creators." *Boston Chronicle* (Aug. 20, 1938).

Photo story on the Three Chocolateers, who introduced the dances peckin' and the skrontch.

1037. "Peg Leg Bates." *New Yorker* (Nov. 20, 1943).

Profiles the one-legged tap dancer.

1038. "Peg Leg Bates Plans to Retire to Club in Country." *Ebony* (May 1955): 67-71.

1039. Percival, John. "John Percival Sees Harlem Return." *Dance and Dancers* (Aug. 1976): 24-25.

Reviews and analyzes the progress of the Dance Theatre of Harlem.

1040.   ———. "Maas Movers at the Oval House, Kensington: Showcase for Black Dancers." *Dance and Dancers* (Oct. 1977): 34-35.

Reviews Maas Movers (the first all-black British professional dance company) debut performance.

1041.   Pereda Valdés, Ildefonso. *Linéa de Color; Ensayos Afro-Americanos.* Santiago de Chile: Ercilla, 1938.

Discusses black traditions and culture in the United States and Latin America in a series of essays, including essays on dance.

1042.   ———. *Negros Esclavos y Negros Libres.* Montevideo: Imprenta "Gaceta Comercial," 1941.

Discusses the blacks of Uruguay historically and sociologically. "Danzas Rioplatenses" (pp. 81-88) describes the calenda, bambula, la chica, and the candombe.

1043.   ———. *El Negro en el Uruguay Pasado y Presente.* Montevideo: Revista del Instituto Histórico y Geográfico del Uruguay, no. 25, 1965.

"Danzas Afrouruguayas" (pp. 149-60) discusses the following dances: calinda, bámbula, la chica, candombe, la semba, and batuque.

1044.   Perry, Claudia. "Exploring the Culture of Harlem." *Florida Times-Union* [Jacksonville, Fla.] (July 25, 1982).

Reviews the exhibit "Black Dance in Photographs" at the Schomburg Center for Research in Black Culture.

1045. Peterson, Stanze. "A Dancer Replies: 'Miz Ann, Please I'd Rather Do It Myself." *The Feet* (June 1973).

States that black experience, which is varied, is a source for black dance. Black is not solely "African" or anything else; all black contributions influence Peterson's choreography.

1046. Pierre, Dorathi Bock. "A Talk with Katherine Dunham." *Educational Dance* (Aug./Sept. 1941): 7-8.

Tells of Dunham's interests in dance, dance education, and anthropology, and of her experiences in the Caribbean as a Rosenwald Fellow.

1047. Pinkney, Alphonso. *Black Americans*. Englewood Cliffs, N.J.: Prentice-Hall, 1969.

Studies the status of blacks in the United States from the beginnings to the 1960s. Chapter 7 summarizes black contributions to dance, stage music, and social values.

1048. Pinnock, Thomas. "Africa-Reggae Dance Theater: A Third World Synthesis." *Dance Book Forum* 1 (1981): 14-15.

Pinnock, a choreographer, discusses a dance theater concert specifically related to the culture of Jamaica.

1049. Pittman, Ken. "Destiné's dance promotes Haiti." *Afro-American* (May 8, 1954): 6.

Profiles Jean-Léon Destiné.

1050. Pitts, George. "New Dance Craze Booms in Miami." *Pittsburgh Courier* [Section 2] (May 26, 1962): 19.

The chicken scratch.

1051. Platt, Orville, H. "Negro Governors." *Papers of the New Haven Colony Historical Society* 6 (1900): 315-35.

Describes the elections of "governors" and "kings" in the eighteenth- and nineteenth- century New England. Describes the parades, dances, music, and costumes accompanying the ceremonies.

1052. "Pneumonia Ends Life of Hemsley Winfield." *New York Amsterdam News* (Jan. 17, 1934).

1053. Pollack, Arthur. "Janet Collins, Golden Dancing Girl of 'Out of this World.'" *Daily Compass* (Jan. 28, 1951).

1054. ———. "Two Dancers Who've Teamed up for an Unusual Program."

Reviews a performance of Donald McKayle dancing with Daniel Nagrin at the Hunter Playhouse, Hunter College, New York City.

1055. "Popular Dances from the Cakewalk to the Watusi." *Ebony* (Aug. 1961): 32-34, 36, 38.

Gives a brief history of black-influenced popular dance in the United States with photographs of Al Minns and Leon James demonstrating such dances as the cakewalk, black bottom, charleston, mess around, and many others.

1056. Porter, Dorothy B. *Afro-Braziliana.* Boston: G.K. Hall, 1978.

Selected works by Afro-Brazilians on Brazilian history and culture. See "Music, Dance and Carnival" pp. 107-19.

1057. "Portfolio of Dance Photographs." *Caribe* 7 (no. 3): 1-20.

Supplements the special issue on dance, *Caribe* 7 (nos. I & II).

1058. "Portrait of a Dancer." *Sepia* (Feb. 1968): 60-64.

Carlton Johnson.

1059.   Poston, Ted. "Drums Boom and Harlem Fades from the Scene."
            New York Post (Mar. 3, 1938).

Describes the Calabar African Dancers, in 1938 the oldest
African dance troupe in the United States.

1060.   ———. "Dancing Away Child Delinquency." *New York Post*
            (June 17, 1947).

Mary Bruce and her dancing school contribute to the end of
delinquency among her pupils.

1061.   Powles, L.D. *Land of the Pink Pearl; or Recollections of Life in
            the Bahamas.* London: Sampson Low, Marston, Searle, and
            Rivington, 1888.

Describes dances and social customs of Nassau society, both
upper and lower crusts.

1062.   "Preserving Folk-Art in Guyana's Culture." *Sunday Graphic*
            [Georgetown, Guyana] (July 23, 1974).

Lavinia Williams and Rajkumarie Singh give their opinions on
folk art in Guyana.

1063.   "Presstime News. Personals: Obituaries." *Dance Magazine* (Jan.
            1968): 10.

Announces the death of Jody Edwards, Butterbeans of the
vaudeville comedy dance act of Butterbeans and Susie.

1064.   "Pretty Los Angeles Dancer Shows Talent in 'South Pacific.'" *Jet*
            (June 19, 1958): 60-61.

Peggy Dave gets dancing role in movie.

1065.   Price, Sally and Richard Price. *Afro-American Arts of the
            Surinam Rain Forest.* Los Angeles: University of California
            Press and Museum of Cultural History, 1980.

A study of the arts of the Surinam rain forest with dancing discussed on pp. 171-74.

1066. Price, Thomas J. "Estado y Necesidades Actuales de las Investigaciones Afro-Colombianas." *Revista Colombiana de Antropología* 2, no. 2 (1954): 11-36.

Reviews the state of Afro-Colombian research and discusses the Afro-Colombian dances cumbia, rumba, bambuco, and others.

1067. Primus, Pearl. "African Dance: Eternity Captured." *Caribe* 7, nos. I & II: 10-13.

1068. ———. "My Statement." *Caribe* 7, nos. I & II: 5. Reprinted from *Black Theater Alliance Newsletter* 4, no. 9 (1979).

1069. ———. "Primitive African Dance (and Its Influence on the Churches of the South)." In *The Dance Encyclopedia* edited by Anatole Chujoy, 387-89. New York: A.S. Barnes, 1949.

Primus compares what she knows of African dance to movements, rhythms, and sounds in southern black churches. Discusses how African dance is directly connected to and preserved in religious expression in southern churches.

1070. ———. "Out of Africa." In *The Dance Has Many Faces* edited by Walter Sorell, 255-58. Cleveland: World Publishing.

Discusses the role of dance in African Culture.

1071. "Private Life of a Chorus Girl." *Our World* (Sept. 1951): 20-23.

On Kathleen Dade, a chorine at New York's Savannah Club.

1072. "Private Life of Josephine Baker." *Our World* (June 1951): 35-42.

1073.   Protzman, Bob. "A Bed-Stuy Talent Reaches the Top." *New York Daily News* (Dec. 18, 1979).

Ben Vereen.

1074.   Puckett, Newbell Niles. *Folk Beliefs of the Southern Negro*. Chapel Hill, N.C.: University of North Carolina, 1926.

Mentions dancing for religious purposes (pp. 60, 543).

1075.   Pyatt, Richard I. "Paul Russell Leaps into Artistic Fulfillment." *Encore American & Worldwide News* (Apr. 18, 1977).

1076.   "Quashie Group of Dancers at Kaufmann Hall." *New York Amsterdam News* (Oct. 29, 1960): 15.

Reviews Mike Quashie and his dancers.

1077.   "Queen of the Dance; Bernice Johnson Has Been 'On Her Toes' since Age Four Now Teaches Dance to 500 Pupils." *Our World* (Mar. 1955): 45-49.

1078.   Rader, Dotson. "Down, but Not Out at the Palace." *Esquire* (June 1974): 80-82, 206-09.

Interviews Josephine Baker and reviews her career.

1079.   Rainer, Peter. "No Maps on My Taps." *Los Angeles Herald Examiner* (Mar. 16, 1979): B-5.

Reviews the film on tap dancing.

1080.   "Rajkumari Marie Bryant." *Our World* (June 1953): 28.

1081.   Ramos, Arthur. *O Folk-lore Negro do Brasil*.   Rio de Janeiro: Livraria-editora da Casa do Estudante do Brasil, 1954.

See Chapter 5, "A Sobrivivência da Dança e da Musica."

1082. Ramos, Diana. "Review of *Black Dance in the United States: from 1619 to 1970* by Lynn Fauley Emery." *Journal of Ethnic Studies* 1, no. 4 (Winter 1974): 116-18.

1083. Ramsey, F., and Charles E. Smith. *Jazzmen.* New York: Harcourt, Brace and Company, 1939.

This history of jazz describes the dances in Congo Square in the chapter on New Orleans music.

1084. Raspberry, William. "Inaugural Gala Offended Some." *Staten Island Advance* (Jan. 27, 1981).

Discusses the controversy surrounding Ben Vereen's performance as Bert Williams at the Presidential Inaugural.

1085. Ravitz, Abe C. "John Pierpont and the Slaves' Christmas." *Phylon* 21, no. 4 (1960): 383-86.

In this excerpt from an unpublished journal, John Pierpont, abolitionist and teacher, describes slaves dancing at a Christmas celebration.

1086. "Raymond Johnson Dances at Pace." *New York Post* (Apr. 8, 1977).

1087. Reboux, Paul. *Le Paradis des Antilles Françaises.* Paris: Librarie de la Revue Française, 1931.

Describes carnival and dancing in "Masques et Tam-Tam" (pp. 71-76).

1088. Redhead, W.A. "Truth, Fact and Tradition in Carriacou." *Caribbean Quarterly* 16, no. 3 (1970): 61-63.

Discusses religious dance festivals in Carriacou.

1089. Rego, Waldeloir. *Capoeira Angola; Ensaio Sócio-Etnografico.* Rio de Janeiro: Companhia Gráfica Lux, 1968.

Gives the origin and analysis of capoeira. Includes the songs and musical instruments used with capoeira.

1090. Reid, Ira DeA. "Mrs. Bailey Pays the Rent." In *Ebony and Topaz* edited by Charles S. Johnson, 144-48. New York: National Urban League, 1927.

Describes rent parties in southern cities and in Harlem.

1091. "Remarkable Production." *The Providence Journal* (Sept. 5, 1934).

Reviews Asadata Dafora's "Kykunkor" at the Casino Theatre in Newport, R.I.

1092. Rhodes, Russell. "A More Humane Mikado Never Did Exist, Believe Us." *New York Herald Tribune* (Apr. 16, 1939).

Profiles Bill Robinson and his performance in the "Hot Mikado."

1093. Rhone, George E. "Curing a Haunted Fiddle." *Keystone Folklore Quarterly* 8 (1963): 81-83.

A ghost story describes a circle dance performed by blacks.

1094. "Rhumba to Vie with Lindy Hop and Truckin.'" *New York Amsterdam News* (Aug. 24, 1935).

1095. "Rhythm Changes with Mood Dancer: Drum Beat like Heart Beat." *Dayton Daily News* (June 28, 1966).

Lavinia Williams conducts dance education clinic for the handicapped.

1096. Ribeiro, Maria de Lourdes Borges. *A Dança do Moçambique.* São Paulo: Ricordi Brasileira, [1959].

1097. ———. "O Baile dos Congos." In *Estudios e Ensaios Folkloricos em Homegem at Renato Almeida* , 639-92. Rio de Janeiro: Ministerio das Relacãos Exteriores, 1960.

Describes examples of congadas and moçambique.

1098. ———. "O Jongo." *Revista do Arquivo Municipal* (São Paulo) 173, and 3 (Jan.-June 1968): 169-238.

About jongo, a religious dance.

1099. Rice, Vernon. "Katherine Dunham." *New York Post* (Apr. 1, 1940).

Reviews Katherine Dunham and her company.

1100. Riley, Clayton. "A 'Train' on the Soul Track." *New York Times* (Feb. 4, 1973).

Discusses the television program "Soul Train," its dances and dancers.

1101. Robb, Marian. "Excellence of Harlem Dance Theatre." *Royal Gazette* (June 20, 1970).

Reviews the Dance Theatre of Harlem performance in Bermuda.

1102. Roberts, John Storm. *Black Music of Two Worlds.* New York: Praeger, 1972.

Surveys black music and dance in the Western Hemisphere. Most dances are discussed in terms of music.

1103. Roberts, W. Adolphe. "Jazz Dancing—A New Color in the American Rainbow." *The Dance Magazine* 12 (May 1929); 26-27, 53.

1104. Robertson, Michael. "Pearl Primus, Ph.D. Returns." *New York Times* (Mar. 18, 1979): Section 2, pp. 28, 34.

Pearl Primus recounts her career past and present.

1105. Robins, Wayne. "Touching Show." *Newsday* (June 26, 1977).

Reviews Ben Vereen at the Westbury Music Fair.

1106. ———. "Dance Review/Sometimes Something New." *Newday* (Sept. 10, 1977).

Reviews performances of Bill T. Jones, Charles Moore, and the Dancers and Drums of Africa performing at the New York Dance Festival.

1107. ———. "No Slack Moments." *Newsday* (Apr. 5, 1978).

Reviews Ben Vereen at the Westbury Music Fair.

1108. "Robinson 'Adopts' Child." *New York Times* (Dec. 14, 1941).

Bill Robinson becomes foster father of an English girl.

1109. Robinson, F.L. "The Coloured People of the United States." *Leisure Hour* 38 (1889): 54-59, 697-700.

Discusses the character of blacks in both the North and the South and describes a cakewalk, clapboard supper, camp meeting, and funeral.

1110. Robinson, Minor. "Biggest Country Resort." *Sepia* (Aug. 1971): 56-64.

Discusses Peg Leg Bates's career and his country resort in the Catskills.

1111. Rodgers, Rod. "For the Celebration of Our Blackness." *Dance Scope* 3, no. 2 (Spring 1967): 6-10.

Discusses the status of black dance and discrimination in the United States.

1112. Rodrigues Molas, Ricardo. "La Música y la danza de los negros en el Buenos Aires de los Siglos XVIII y XIX." *Historia; Revista Trimestral de Historia Argentina, Americana y Española* 2, no. 7 (Jan-Mar. 1957): 103-26.

1113. Roehrs, Jane. "The Teacher Can Make It Look So Easy." *The Charlotte News* [N.C.] (Jan. 28, 1972).

Raymond Johnson teaches a class in his duties as affiliate artist at the University of North Carolina at Charlotte.

1114. "Ron Davis Dancers." *New York Times* (June 5, 1967).

Reviews the New York Debut of the Ron Davis Dancers at the Cheetah discotheque.

1115. Rosen, Lillie F. "Eugene Von Grona." *Wisdom's Child* [N.Y.] (Nov. 23, 1981).

1116. ———. "Von Grona and His First American Negro Ballet." *Dance News* (Mar. 1982).

Reviews a revival performance.

1117. ———. "National Dance Theatre Co. of Jamaica." *Attitudes* 2, no. 6 (Nov. 1983): 5-6.

1118. Rosenwald, Peter J. "New Vistas for Black Dance." *Wall Street Journal* (Oct. 2, 1972).

Surveys the growth of black dance companies. Mentions the George Faison University Dance Experience, Inner City Repertory Company, and Black Dance Theater Ensemble.

1119. ———. "Harlem's Street-Wise Dance Company." *Wall Street Journal* (Jan. 9, 1981).

Analyzes the Dance Theatre of Harlem's work, its economic situation, and its financial management.

1120. ———. "'Equus' Overpowers the Beasts in 'Magic Flute.'" *Wall Street Journal* (Jan. 26, 1982).

Reviews the Dance Theatre of Harlem's première of "Equus" called a "mature step in a new direction." This step is compared to the one taken at the same time by the New York City Ballet with "Magic Flute."

1121. Rossi, Vicente. *Cosas de Negros*. 2nd ed. Buenos Aires: Libreria Hachette, 1958. Original ed. ca. 1926.

Gives the origins of various dances: "El primer candombes" (pp. 50-59), "El Tango" (pp. 143-56), and "Los Milagros del Tango" (pp. 157-79).

1122. Ross, Leonard Q. [Leo Calvin Rosten]. *The Strangest Places*. New York: Harcourt Brace, 1939.

Describes the Savoy Ballroom on pp. 179-91.

1123. Rowe, Billy. "Clarence Robinson Dead at 79." *New York Amsterdam News* (Sept. 8, 1979): 43.

Clarence Robinson started as a dancer in choruses; he later became a renown impresario and choreographer who produced shows in the original Cotton Club and on the east coast circuit of Philadelphia, New York, and Washington, D.C.

1124. "Ruby Richards: The Gal Who Took Paris." *Our World* (Apr. 1954): 78-82.

Formerly known as Curlytop at the Cotton Club, this *Folies Bergere* star takes her act to New York's Latin Quarter.

1125. "Rumba Was a Native Cuban Dance." *Afro-American* (July 11, 1931).

1126. Ryan, Marion. "The City of the Dance." *World's Record* (Mar. 15, 1921).

   Describes the celebration of Cuban Independence Day, including the dances.

1127. [S., B.) B.S. "Hadassah, Premice and Primus." *Dance Observer* (Feb. 1945): 21.

1128. [S., N.] N.S. "Twentieth Anniversary for Urban League." *New York Times* (Mar. 21, 1938).

   American Negro Ballet in a benefit for the New York Urban League at Town Hall in New York City.

1129. [S., R.] R.S. "Helen McGehee, and Ronne Aul." *Dance Observer* 18 (May 1951): 72-73.

   Reviews joint recital given at YM-YWHA, Apr. 7, 1951.

1130. Saal, Herbert. "Woman in Flight." *Newsweek* 79 (May 1, 1972): 66-67.

   Judith Jamison.

1131. ———. "On Their Toes." *Newsweek* (Apr. 29, 1974).

   Dance Theatre of Harlem and its school.

1132. Sabin, Robert. "La Danse aux U.S.A." *Formes et Couleurs* 6 (1947): n.p.

   Gives overview of major American dance activities, including Pearl Primus and Katherine Dunham.

1133. Salaam, Yusef A. *Capoeira; African Brazilian Karate.* N.p.: n.p., 1983.

1134. Sales, Aishah. "'Sandman'—Tops in Tap." *New York Amsterdam News* (July 12, 1980): 35.

Covers the career and dancing style of Sandman Sims.

1135. Salisbury, Wilma. "Dancing Doctor Takes a Giant Step." *The Feet* (June 1973): 19.

Discusses Ernest L. Washington, M.D., and his specialty in dance orthopedics.

1136. "Salome." *Our World* (Dec. 1950): 24-26.

Carmen De Lavallade stars in a Lester Horton work.

1137. Sanderson, Ivan T. "The History of Jazz Dance." Parts 1, 2, 3. *The Dancing Times* (Jan., Feb., Mar. 1935): 454-56; 566-67; 676-77.

1138. Savage, Nancy. "Raven Wilkinson Talks of Her Achievement in the World of Ballet." *The Tribune* [Nassau] (Sept. 11, 1965).

Raven Wilkinson was the first black ballerina with a white company, the Ballet Russes de Monte Carlo.

1139. "Savoy Story." *Our World* (June 1951): 20-25.

Highlights 25 years of the Savoy Ballroom. Includes photos.

1140. "Say Harlem Is Home of Dance Craze, 'Suzie-Q.'" *Chicago Defender* (Dec. 12, 1936).

Discusses the origin of the Suzie-Q.

1141. "Says Negro Began Tango." *New York Times* (Oct. 28, 1928).

1142. "Scarsdale Reports No Reds in Schools." *New York Times* (Apr. 24, 1953).

After reviewing several books and school programs including a Pearl Primus performance at an assembly, a committee of the Scarsdale Town Club ruled there was no Communist infiltration.

1143. Scarupa, Harriet Jackson. "Claire Haywood and Doris Jones—Pioneers in Ballet." *Essence* 6 (Jan. 1976): 64-65, 80, 92-93, 95.

Discusses the history of the Jones-Haywood School in Washington, D.C. Describes the teachers' dedication to their students.

1144. Scher, Valerie. "Alvin Ailey: From Disco Dreamland to Adorable Zombies." *Chicago Sun-Times* (Feb. 27, 1981).

Reviews a performance of "Phases," "Astral Traveling," "Steel Point," and "Later that Day" at Chicago's Auditorium Theater.

1145. Schuler, Monica. "Myalism and the African Religious Tradition in Jamaica." In *Africa and the Caribbean: The Legacies of a Link* edited by Margaret E. Crahan and Franklin W. Knight, 65-79. Baltimore: Johns Hopkins University Press, 1979.

1146. Schultz, Christian. *Travels on an Inland Voyage.* 2 vols. New York: Isaac Riley, 1810.

Describes the dancing, costumes, and musical instruments of New Orleans (vol. 2, p. 197).

1147. Schumach, Murray. "Bill Robinson and 300 Friends Hail His Birthday on Hudson Cruise." *New York Times* (May 25, 1948).

1148. Seabrook, W.B. *The Magic Island.* New York: Harcourt, Brace and Company, 1929.

Relates his experiences with the various religious activities in Haiti. Seabrook participated in and describes voodoo ceremonies, including the dancing.

1149.   Seaga, Edward. "Revival Cults in Jamaica." *Jamaica Journal* 3, no.2 (1969): 3-13.

Gives the characteristics and rituals of the Pocomania and Zion Revival cults in Jamaica.

1150.   Seale, Lea and Marianna Seale. "Easter Rock: A Louisiana Negro Ceremony." *Journal of American Folklore* (Oct./Dec. 1942): 212-18.

Describes a procession done with a "double-shuffle dance step." The procession is done on Easter in a midnight-till-sunrise service.

1151.   Sealy, Joan. "Ballet Star Tells of Pain, Triumph that Defines Dance." *News World* (May 20, 1982).

Interviews Donna Wood, lead dancer with Alvin Ailey's company.

1152.   Seaman, Julian. "Jungle Dances." *New York Daily Mirror* (May 19, 1934).

Reviews Asadata Dafora's "Kykunkor" on opening night at the Unity Theater.

1153.   Sears, Art, Jr. "Two Different Worlds Find Happiness in Marriage." *Jet* (Nov. 12, 1964): 46-50.

Chubby Checker at home with his Dutch wife.

1154.   Segal, Lewis. "'Tap II' at UCLA's Royce Hall." *Los Angeles Times* (Dec. 24, 1979): Part 4, p. 11.

Reviews tap program featuring Honi Coles, Howard "Sandman" Sims, Foster Johnson, and the Nicholas Brothers.

1155.   Seldes, Gilbert. "Shake Your Feet." *New Republic* 44 (Nov. 4, 1925): 283-84.

Expresses enthusiasm over the charleston as a theatrical dance and as a social dance.

1156.   "Seven in the Spotlight." *Encore* (May 17, 1976): 24.

Includes Curt Davis and Karen Burke, in the Fred Benjamin Dance Company.

1157.   "Sexiest Stripper of Them All." *Color* (Apr. 1954): 45-48.

Pictures a strip routine done by dancer Betty Brisbane.

1158.   "Shake Dancers; Their Private Life." *Our World* (Oct. 1953): 74.

1159.   "Shakin' Apples." *New York Post* (Dec. 8, 1937).

Adelaide Hall introduces the canned apple, a combination of the can can and the big apple.

1160.   Shaw, Ellen. "It's the Conga Drum Now Instead of Booze and Junk." *The Sunday Bulletin* [Philadelphia] (Oct. 21, 1973).

Discusses the work of Ile Ife Black Humanitarian Center and the Arthur Hall Afro-American Dance Ensemble of Philadelphia.

1161.   Shawn, Ted. "Black Christmas." *Dance Magazine* (May 1950): 27-29, 34.

Ted Shawn recounts his visit to Haiti at Christmas to learn about Haitian dance and to observe Jean-Léon Destiné and the National Folklore Company of Haiti.

1162.   "She Teaches Ballet to Tots." *Hue* (Feb. 1958): 54-55.

Lavinia Williams teaches in Haiti.

1163.   Shedd, Margaret. "Carib Dance Patterns." *Theatre Arts Monthly* 7, no. 1 (1933): 65-77.

Describes a John Canoe festival in detail.

1164. "Sheldon Hoskins Buried in Philly." *New York Amsterdam News* (Apr. 26, 1958): 4.

Choreographed the Broadway production of "Carmen Jones."

1165. "Sheldon Hoskins, Noted Ballet Master, Buried." *Afro-American* (May 3, 1958): 18.

1166. Shelton, Suzanne. "Michel Fokine's 'Schéhérazade.'" *Dance Magazine* (Jan. 1981): 74-81.

Discusses how the Dance Theatre of Harlem prepared for the revival of this well-known work.

1167. Shepard, Joan. "Dance Group Has Roots in 1937 Harlem." *New York News* (Nov. 29, 1981).

Gives a short history of the first American Negro Ballet and discusses Eugene Von Grona and his revival of that company.

1168. Shepard, Richard F. "Dancemobile's First Stop: 134th Off Lenox." *New York Times* (July 27, 1967): 28.

1169. ——. "Afro-Folkloric Troupe Opens Talent Fete." *New York Times* (Apr. 23, 1969).

Reviews of Afro-American Folkloric Troupe.

1170. "Show Business' Newest Ellington." *Ebony* (Dec. 1963): 67-71, 73, 75.

Mercedes Ellington (Duke's granddaughter) is "first Negro dancer to win a spot in the Jackie Gleason Show's famed June Taylor chorus line."

1171. Siegel, Marcia B. *At the Vanishing Point.* New York: Saturday Review Press, 1972.

Section III, "Black Dance: A New Separation" (pp. 137-73), discusses Siegel's attempts to deal with problems she finds in criticizing black dance performances, and enumerates her principles for judging black dance.

1172. Silverman, Jill. "A New Step for a Ballet Soloist." *New York Times* (Mar. 18, 1979).

Profiles Paul Russell, formerly of Dance Theatre of Harlem, then principal dancer of the Scottish Ballet, prior to a performance with the Massapequa Symphony Orchestra.

1173. ———. "Hoofers Are on Tap in a Movie Première." *New York Times* (Jan. 31, 1982).

Discusses Letitia Jay's efforts to revive tap dancing.

1174. ———. "Bill T. Jones and Arnie Zane." *Andy Warhol's Interview* (Oct. 1984).

Profiles two choreographers who use an "assortment of movement styles, emotional visual imagery."

1175. Simond, Ike. *Old Slack's Reminiscences and Pocket History of the Colored Profession from 1865 to 1891*. Bowling Green, Ohio: Popular Press, 1974.

Names the important black minstrels and other performers of the nineteenth century. Simond, a performer himself, saw most of these people perform.

1176. Simpson, George Eaton. "Peasant Songs and Dances of Northern Haiti." *Journal of Negro History* 25 (1940) 203-15.

Discusses the occasions when various songs and dances are performed.

1177. ———. "Four Vodun Ceremonies." *Journal of American Folklore* 59 (Apr.-June 1946): 154-67.

1178. ———. "Two Vodun-Related Ceremonies." *Journal of American Folklore* 61 (Jan.-Mar. 1948): 49-52.

1179. Sinclair, Abiola. "Break Dancing: From the Street to the Ritz." *New York Amsterdam News* (Oct. 8, 1983): 30.

1180. Sissle, Noble. "How Jo Baker Got Started. *Negro Digest* (Aug. 1951): 15-19.

Josephine Baker's story is told by one of the first people who helped her in her career.

1181. "Six Indiana Students to Study Ethnic Dance." *Chicago Defender* (May 25, 1976): 13.

Six members of the Indiana University Afro-American Dance Company leave for N.Y. to study with Arthur Mitchell and the Chuck Davis Company.

1182. "Skilled Negro Ballet Dancers Helping Broadway Integration." *Jet* (Apr. 17, 1958): 60-61.

1183. Small, Linda. "Black Dancer/Black Traveler." *Dance Magazine* 53 (Oct. 1979): 78-81.

Reviews the performances of the works of various choreographers such as Eleo Pomare, Dinizulu, and Garth Fagan. Includes thoughts on black dance criticism and the audiences at black dance performances. Discusses a definition of black dance.

1184. Smiley, Portia. "Foot Wash in Alabama and North Carolina." *Southern Workman* 25 (Apr. 1896): 101, 102.

Each of the foot-wash rituals described is followed by a ring shout.

1185. Smith, Art. "Bill (Bojangles) Robinson Dead." *New York Daily News* (Nov. 26, 1949).

1186. Smith, Cecil. "West Indian Drumbeat." *New York Times Book Review* (July 18, 1948).

Reviews Earl Leaf's *Isles of Rhythm.*

1187. Smith, Ernie. "Recollections and Reflections of a Jazz Dance Film Collector." *Dance Research Journal* 15, no. 2 (Spring 1983): 46-48.

A major collector.

1188. Smith, J. Murray. "How One American Fares Abroad." *Chicago Defender* (Sept. 1, 1934).

Profiles Buddy Bradley who left the United States to get the recognition he sought.

1189. Smith, Joseph Hutchinson. "Folksongs of the Ameircan Negro." *Sewanee Review* 32 (1924): 206-24.

Discusses the African origins of black songs and hymns mainly, but mentions dances such as the shout, calinda, conjai, and Jonah's ban' in relation to the songs sung with them.

1190. Smith, M.G. "A Note on Truth, Fact and Tradition in Carriacou." *Caribbean Quarterly* , nos. 3-4 (1971): 128-38.

1191. Smith, Wayne C. "Danish Ballerina Makes American Debut in Becket." *Springfield Union* [Springfield, Mass.] (Aug. 21, 1954).

Also reviews Aubrey Hitchin's Negro Dance Theatre, the all-male ballet troupe.

1192. Snelson, Floyd G. "Broadway Bound." *Pittsburgh Courier* (Jan. 9, 1932).

Profiles Bill Robinson.

1193. ———. "Louise (Jota) Cooke Première Nite Club Danseuse." *Pittsburgh Courier* (June 4, 1932).

1194. Sodré, Muniz. *Samba o Dono do Corpo; Ensaios.*   Rio de
Janeiro: Editora Codeiri, 1979.

Essays discuss samba and dance in a cultural context.
Illustrated with photographs and drawings.

1195. Solien, Nancie L. "West Indian Characteristics of the Black
Carib." *Southwestern Journal of Anthropology* 15 (1959):
300-08.

The similarities of the Black Carib of Honduras to the West
Indies are elucidated. The dances described are the punta of the
Caribs, the Haitian point, and the John Canoe of the West Indies.

1196. Solomons, Gus, Jr. "An Elegance Is Implied." *DanceScope* 3,
no. 2 (Spring 1967): 11-16.

Attempts to answer the questions "What is black dance?" and
"How does being black influence your dancing?"

1197. Sommer, Sally R. "Sugar Sullivan." *Village Voice* (Apr. 1,
1981): 66-68.

Sketches the life of a Savoy lindy hopper and the lindy
champion of the Harvest Moon Ball, 1955.

1198. Sorrell, Walter. *The Dance through the Ages.*   New York:
Grosset and Dunlap, 1967.

Chapter 18, "Jazz and the Negro Dance," summarizes black
dance in the United States.

1199. ———. "Rod Rodgers Dance Company, Clark Center, N.Y. Dec.
12-13, 1970." *Dance News* (Feb. 1971): 5, 16.

Performed "Now! Nigga," "Sketches," "Dances in Projected
Space."

1200. "SOS." *New York Times* (Aug. 28, 1960).

States that Edna Guy, early concert dancer, was working at the
New York State Training School for Girls, Hudson, N.Y.

1201. Southern, Eileen. *The Music of Black Americans: A History.*
New York: W.W. Norton, 1971.

A history of black music that intersperses brief bits of dance
history, such as slave dancing, minstrelsy, the cakewalk, and juba.

1202. Spaulding, H.G. "Under the Palmetto." *Continental Monthly* 4
(Aug. 1863): 188-203.

Describes life on the Sea Islands, S.C., during the Civil War.
Describes a ring shout (pp. 196-97.)

1203. "Speaking of People." *Ebony* (Aug. 1974): 6.

Brief biography of Claude Brooks, age five, dancing with the
Dance Theatre of Harlem.

1204. Speers, Mary Walker Finley. "Negro Songs and Folklore."
Journal of American Folklore 23 (1910): 435-39.

Sketchily describes a dance done to two songs collected from
blacks living in Chesapeake.

1205. "Spreadin, Rhythm Around." *Life* (Dec. 28, 1936): 30, 31.

Photo story on lindy hopping.

1206. "Spring Dream." *Headlines and Pictures* (Aug. 1945): 48.

Announces that Janet Collins was granted a Rosenwald
Fellowship. Also gives a brief review of her career.

1207. "Square Dance Caller." *Ebony* (June 1954): 55-61.

Profiles Jesse Cosby of Waterloo, Iowa, who teaches square
dancing.

1208. Stahl, Norma Gengal. "The First Lady of the Metropolitan Opera Ballet." *Dance Magazine* (Feb. 1954): 27-29.

Interviews Janet Collins.

1209. Stanton, Ali. "Mme. Lavinia Williams: A Dunham Pioneer." *New York Amsterdam News* (Apr. 11, 1981).

1210. ———. "Mary Bruce's Starbuds, A Harlem Institution." *New York Amsterdam News* (June 12, 1982): 29.

Profiles Mary Bruce, the long-time Harlem dance teacher, and her students, the Starbuds.

1211. "Ruth Williams Dance Students Learn Life Discipline." *New York Amsterdam News* (June 12, 1982): 40.

Profiles a long-time Harlem dance teacher.

1212. Start, Clarissa. "Bill Robinson Still Stepping High at 70." *St. Louis Post-Dispatch* (Apr. 12, 1949).

1213. Stearns, Marshall and Jean Stearns. "Williams and Walker and the Beginnings of Vernacular Dance of Broadway." *Keystone Folklore Quarterly* 11, no. 1 (1966): 3-11.

1214. ———. "Frontiers of Humor: American Vernacular Dance." *Southern Folklore Quarterly* 30 (Sept. 1966): 227-35.

Gives a brief history of black humor and comedy dance teams. The teams discussed are Stringbeans and Sweetie May, Butterbeans and Susie, Stump and Stumpy, Cook and Brown.

1215. ———. "Vernacular Dance in Musical Comedy; Harlem Takes the Lead." *New York Folklore Quarterly* 22, no. 4 (Dec. 1966): 251-61.

Discusses the importance of the "Darktown Follies" in the history of the black theater in the United States. "Darktown Follies" opened in 1913 at the LaFayette Theater in Harlem.

1216. ———. *The Jazz Dance; the Story of American Vernacular Dance.* New York: Macmillan, 1968.

Gives the history of American vernacular dance, including social dance and tap dance. Includes anecdotes and interviews with surviving dancers. All major dancers and dance teams are featured.

1217. "Steps in Time—A Tap-Dance Festival." *New York Times* (Dec. 28, 1979): C1, C11.

1218. Stone, Chuck. "Philadanco's Dazzling Success Also Hurts." *Philadelphia Daily News* (July 17, 1977): 12.

1219. Stoop, Norma McLain. "Reviewing the Tube: 'Poppy.'" *Dance Magazine* (Nov. 1971): 102.

Reviews the George Faison Universal Dance Experience performing on "Soul," Oct. 6, 1971.

1220. ———. "All the World's a Stage for Clive Thompson of the Alvin Ailey American Dance Theatre." *Dance Magazine* (Oct. 1978): 78-85.

1221. ———. "Dancing to the Duke." *Dance Magazine* (Mar. 1981): 54-57.

Reviews Broadway musical "Sophisticated Ladies."

1222. Strouse, Richard. "At 70, Still Head Hoofer." *New York Times Magazine* (May 23, 1948).

"Bill Robinson confounds doctors and dances superbly as ever."

1223. Stroyer, Jacob. *My Life in the South.* New and enlarged ed. Salem, Mass.: Newcomb and Gauss, 1898.

Former slave's memories, including Christmas celebrations.

1224. Sudol, Valerie. "Institute Welds Arts with Education." *Star-Ledger* [Newark, N.J.] (July 29, 1979).

Chuck Davis gives his thoughts about education and the artist, and his being a part of the Artist-Teacher Institute held at Fort Hancock, Gateway National Park.

1225. ———. "Chuck Davis Pulsates with Primal Energy." *The Star-Ledger* [Newark, N.J.] (Sept. 29, 1979).

1226. Sullivan, Dan. "Harlem Has Real Dancing in the Streets." *New York Times* (June 28, 1967).

The Harlem Cultural Festival starts with a street dance.

1227. Sullivan, Ed. "Broadway: Tops in Taps." *New York Daily News* (Dec. 15, 1936).

Celebrities give celebration honoring Bill Robinson's 50th anniversary in show business.

1228. ———. "Little Old New York: Nature Boy." *New York Daily News* (May 23, 1948).

Profiles Bill Robinson.

1229. Sullivan, Edward S. "Negro Ballet Exotic, Unique." *Los Angeles Examiner* (Feb. 26, 1951).

Reviews the Hollywood Negro Ballet.

1230. Supree, Burt. "Any Two Men on the Planet." *Village Voice* (Mar. 18, 1981).

Interviews Bill T. Jones and Arnie Zane, dance duo and choreographers.

1231. Swartz, Paul. "Voodoo, Black Magic of Cuban Dance." *Coronet* (June 1938).

Describes dances such as diabolito, shoeing the mare, fruit vendor, and flea-killer done by Cuba's Nañigo cult.

1232. "Sweet Charity's Exciting Paula Kelly." *Sepia* (May 1967): 24-26.

1233. "Swing Music and Popular Dance." *Dance Herald* (Feb. 1938).

1234. Syse, Glenna. "Alvin Ailey Artists: Reaching for Infinity with Pride and Punch." *Chicago Sun-Times* (Feb. 25, 1981).

Reviews the Alvin Ailey American Dance Theater performing "Memoria," "Rainbow 'Round My Shoulder," and "Revelations" at Chicago's Auditorium Theater.

1235. Szwed, John F. and Roger D. Abrahams. *Afro-American Folk Culture: An Annotated Bibliography of Materials from North, Central and South America and the West Indies.* Philadelphia: Institute for the Study of Human Issues, 1978.

1236. [T., W.] W.T. "Hot Night for Jazz Dance." *New York Herald Tribune* (June 22, 1964).

1237. Talbot, George A. "Pictorial Essay." In *Afro-American Anthropology: Contemporary Perspectives* edited by Norman E. Whitten, Jr. and John F. Szwed. New York: Free Press, 1970.

Thirty-two pages of photographs illustrate different aspects of black-American culture, including music, rituals, dance.

1238. Talese, Gay. "Harlem for Fun." *Esquire* 58 (Sept. 1962): 135-42.

Discusses the revival of white interest in Harlem nightlife and focuses on the twist.

1239. Tallant, Robert. *Voodoo in New Orleans.* New York: Macmillan, 1946.

This history of voodoo in New Orleans describes dancing in voodoo ceremonies.

1240. "Tallest Girl in Show Business." *Hue* (Nov. 1954): 32-35.

Princess R'Wanda née Laura Lewis, former Dunham dancer, turns to strip-tease.

1241. "Tap Dancer Bill Bailey, Pearl's Brother, Dies." *Jet* (Jan. 4, 1979): 61.

1242. "Tap Dancer Turned Preacher." *Ebony* (Aug. 1950): 59-65.

Features Bill Bailey as a preacher.

1243. "Tap Dancing Negro Now Widely Sought Once Ran Elevator." *New York Herald Tribune* (Jan. 5, 1930).

Billy Pierce, teacher of dance to Broadway stars.

1244. Tapley, Mel. "Mary Bruce's Starbuds Will Bloom at Edison Theatre." *New York Amsterdam News* (June 11, 1977): D-11.

1245. ———. "Percival Borde Dies Suddenly." *New York Amsterdam News* (Sept. 8, 1979): 25.

1246. ———. "That Hines Kid: Entertainment's 47 Varieties." *New York Amsterdam News* (Sept. 22, 1979): 27.

Discusses both Maurice and Gregory Hines but emphasizes Gregory, then appearing on Broadway in "Sophisticated Ladies."

1247. ———. "Harlem Dance Teachers Extraordinaire." *New York Amsterdam News* (May 16, 1981): 37.

Profiles Mary Bruce and Ruth Williams, two long-time dance teachers.

1248. ———. "The Hines Brothers: Kicking up Their Heels, Coast to Coast, in 'Sophisticated Ladies.'" *New York Amsterdam News* (Jan. 9, 1982): 19.

1249. ———. "Charles Moore: A Performer who Does Research." *New York Amsterdam News* (Nov. 13, 1982): 36.

1250. Terry, Bruce. "Dance Festival of Solos and Duos Honors Mentor Thelma Hill." *Grafica* (Mar. 21, 1982).

Sketches Thelma Hill and her career with a review of the performance honoring her. The artists performing: Loretta Abbott, Thea Barnes, Stanley Bates, Marla Bingham, Dianne McIntyre, John Parks, Amani Payne, Mark Rubin, Warren Spears, Rima Vette, and Clyde Wilder.

1251. Terry, Walter. "A Collaboration that Had to Happen: Hugh Masekela and Alvin Ailey." *Topic* , issue no. 54: 13-15.

On "Masekela Language," Ailey, Masekela, and the possibility of their further collaboration.

1252. ———. "To the Negro Dance." *New York Herald Tribune* (Jan. 28, 1940).

Reviews Agnes DeMille's "Black Ritual" choreographed for Ballet Theater.

1253. ———. "Dafora's African Group Stages a Dance Drama of Tribal Life." *New York Herald Tribune* (Apr. 9, 1940).

Describes and reviews "Zunguru," performed at the Chanin Auditorium, New York City, Apr. 8, 1940.

1254. ——. "Reflections on Bond between African, Western Dance Forms." *New York Herald Tribune* (Nov. 2, 1941).

Compares the dancing of Asadata Dafora's dancers in "Batanga" and Allyn McLerie and John Butler's dancing in the Cotillion Room of the Hotel Pierre.

1255. ——. "Jacob's Pillow Festival." *New York Herald Tribune* (July 15, 1953).

Includes Donald McKayle and his company performing "Games" and "Nocturne."

1256. ——. "Dance: Voodoo Ceremony." *New York Herald Tribune* (July 10, 1955).

1257. ——. "Voodoo for Theater Developed in Haiti." *New York Herald Tribune* (July 17, 1955).

1258. ——. "Met's Ballet." *New York Herald Tribune* (Oct. 14, 1956).

Reviews Geoffrey Holder's dance performance in "Aida."

1259. ——. "Petrouchka Returns." *Saturday Review* (Apr. 11, 1970): 41.

Reviews the Joffrey Ballet's performance of "Petrouchka," with Christian Holder dancing the Blackamoor.

1260. ——. *Dance in America.* New York: Harper and Row, 1971.

The chapter "The Black Dance" (pp. 156-64) gives an overview of the history of black dance in the United States.

1261. "Thanks to Doug Crutchfield Fru Nilsen Can Dance." *Ebony* (Apr. 1970): 86-91.

A Cincinnati-born dancer, Crutchfield teaches dance to Copenhagen's old and disabled people.

1262. "Thelma Hill Dies of Smoke Inhalation at Age 53." *New York Times* (Nov. 23, 1977): B2

1263. "These Legs Have Danced 5000 Miles; Hortense Allen Has Climbed the Chorus to Success." *Our World* (Oct. 1951): 33-35.

1264. "$13,500 Gift to Aid Jazz Dance School." *New York Times* (June 21, 1965).

The Ron Davis Modern-Jazz Dance Workshop and the Ron Davis Dance Company receive a three-year grant.

1265. Thompson, Robert Farris. "Palladium Mambo I." *Dance Magazine* 33 (Sept. 1959): 73-75.

Analyzes mambo dancers of the Palladium Ballroom who developed a unique style of the mambo.

1266. ———. "Palladium Mambo II." *Dance Magazine* 33 (Nov. 1959): 70-71.

Describes the merger of jazz and black-Cuban influences that made the mambo unique. Also analyzes the moves and self-choreography of two star couples of the Palladium ballroom doing the mambo.

1267. ———. "Enter Cuban Pete and Millie." *Ballroom Dance Magazine* (Jan. 1961): 16-17, 26.

Gives biography of a stylistically influential pair of New York mambo dancers.

1268. ———. "Portrait of the Pachanga." *Saturday Review* 44 (Oct. 28, 1961): 42-43, 54. Reprinted in *Caribe* 7, nos. I & II: 47-49.

Gives the elements of the pachanga, its development in Cuba, and its relation to Afro-Cuban music before becoming a popular dance.

1269. Thompson, Ruth. "Ben Vereen, His Roots...and Ben Vereen Himself." *The Trib* [New York] (Feb. 10, 1978).

1270. Thompson, U.S. "Florence Mills." In *Negro Anthology, 1931-1933* edited by Nancy Cunard, 320-21. London: Wishart, 1934.

1271. "Throng Bids Bojangles Adieu." *New York World-Telegram* (Nov. 28, 1949).

1272. "Throngs Mourn for Berry." *New York Amsterdam News* (Oct. 13, 1951): 3.

Ananias Berry of the Berry Brothers dies.

1273. Tigre, Hector Bastos. "Carnival in Brazil." *Bulletin of the Pan-American Union* (Nov. 1939): 649-51.

1274. Tinker, Edward Larocque. *Toucoutou.* New York: Dodd, Mead and Co., 1928.

This novel of quadroon life in New Orleans includes descriptions of the bamboula, calinda, counjaille, and dancing in Place Congo.

1275. ———. *Creole City.* New York: Longmans, Green and Co., 1953.

Describes life in New Orleans. Also includes a discussion of black dance.

1276. Todd, Arthur. "Four Centuries of American Dance: The Negro Folk Dance in America." *Dance Magazine* 24 (Jan. 1950): 14-15, 41.

1277. ———. "Four Centuries of American Dance: Theatre Dance Before the American Revolution, 1734-1775." *Dance Magazine* 24 (Mar. 1950): 20-21, 35.

Briefly describes the first "Negro dance" done in blackface in
Philadelphia.

1278.   ———. "Four Centuries of American Dance: Negro-American
Theatre Dance, 1840-1900." *Dance Magazine* 24 (Nov.
1950): 20-21, 33-34.

Discusses the beginnings of minstrelsy, vaudeville, cakewalk,
and Williams and Walker.

1279.   ———. "Dance: Riches: The Art of the American Negro Is One of
Our Foremost National Treasures." *New York Times* (July 2,
1961).

Discusses some of the major black modern dancers such as
Katherine Dunham, Pearl Primus, Janet Collins, Carmen De
Lavallade, Alvin Ailey, James Truitte, Talley Beatty, Louis
Johnson, Donald McKayle, Matt Turney, and Mary Hinkson.
Also gives a history of black dance from slavery to modern times.

1280.   ———. "American Negro Dance: A National Treasure." *The
Ballet Annual* 16 (1962): 92-105.

Surveys the history of black dance in the United States from
slavery to modern times.

1281.   ———. "A Look at Lightning." *Dance and Dancers* (May 1962):
13-14.

Reviews the Martha Graham Dance Company, with Matt
Turney performing.

1282.   ———. "Two Way Passage for Dance." *Dance Magazine* 36 (July
1962): 39-41.

Discusses Alvin Ailey Dance Theater's tour of Australia and the
Far East in 1962 as the first all-black dance company to have been
sent abroad in the President's International Exchange Program.

1283. Toll, Robert C. *Blacking Up; the Minstrel Show in Nineteenth-Century America.* New York: Oxford University Press, 1974.

Relates how minstrelsy became the most popular entertainment in the United States. Discusses minstrel dances such as the buck and wing, patting juba, ring shout, and the shuffle. Also mentions Billy Kersands, famous for popularizing the dance Essence of Old Virginia.

1284. "Tornado from Trinidad." *Time* (May 6, 1957): 42.

Profiles Geoffrey Holder.

1285. Traguth, Fred. *Modern Jazz Dance.* Bonn: Verlag Dance Motion, [1977].

Jazz dance technique in photos.

1286. Tutt, J. Homer. "In Defense of the Mayor of Harlem: Bill Robinson Urged Not to Quit Office." *Afro-American* (Nov. 21, 1936).

1287. "Twist Banned in Egypt." *Chicago Defender* (Dec. 28, 1962): 3.

1288. "Two Dancers Die at Ripe Age." *Dance News* (Jan. 1950): 11.

Obituary of Dora Dean of the team Johnson and Dean, who introduced the cakewalk to New York in 1895. (The other obituary is of a white dancer.)

1289. "Two Fans and a Body, Jean Idell, Sepia Sally Rand." *Our World* (Aug. 1952): 54-55.

This successful strip-tease dancer started as one of Mary Bruce's Starbuds.

1290. "Two Star Wedding." *Our World* (Oct. 1955): 8-15.

Carmen De Lavallade and Geoffrey Holder wed in Westport, Conn.

1291. "U-I Film Planned on Bill Robinson." *New York Times* (Aug. 15, 1955).

1292. Utrecht, L. "Nationaal Ballet Met Drie Premières de Vuurvogel Nog Boeiend." *Algemeen Handelsblad* (Dec. 12, 1967).

Review of Het Nationaal Ballet, Netherlands. Mentions Raven Wilkinson.

1293. Van Vechten, Carl. *Parties.* 1930. Reprint. New York: Avon, 1977.

A novel of the Harlem scene in the 1920s. Describes the lindy hop (pp. 157-61).

1294. Vaughan, David. "Morse Donaldson Dance Theatre, Negro Ensemble Company Dance and Music Festival. St. Mark's Playhouse, N.Y.C., March 27-30, 1973." *Dance Magazine* (June 1973): 67-68.

1295. Vega, Hector. "The Bomba and Plena: Africa Retained in Music and Dance of Puerto Rico." *Caribe* 7 (nos. I & II): 43.

1296. Velásquez, M. Rogerio. "La Fiesta de los Negritos de Nóvita." *Boletín Cultural y Bibliográfico* 4, no. 9 (1961): 859-60.

Describes a folk festival of the Afro-Colombian population of the city of Nóvita, including roles, dress, dances, and music.

1297. Victor, Metta Victoria Fuller. *Maum Guinea and Her Plantation "Children": A Story of Christmas Week with the American Slaves.* London and New York: Beadle, n.d.

This fictionalized account of plantation life describes the slaves' dances, music, and religious beliefs.

1298. Vines, Richard Eyre. "Maas Movers." *The Dancing Times* (Sept. 1977): 697.

Reviews the debut performance of Britain's first all-black dance company in July 1977.

1299. "*Vogue* Covers the Town: American Negro Ballet." *Vogue* (Dec. 15, 1937): 27.

Profiles and reviews the American Negro Ballet.

1300. "Voodoo Goes to College." *Ebony* (July 1952): 75-78.

Vera Duncan, former Dunham dancer, teaches traditional dance at Roosevelt College, Chicago, Ill.

1301. [W., E.] E.W. "Blij Weerzien met 'De Vuurvogel.'" *De Telegraaf* (Dec. 12, 1967).

Reviews the Nationaal Ballet of Nederlands dancing "Firebird" and "Four Temperaments." Mentions Raven Wilkinson briefly.

1302. [W., J.] J.W. "Outstanding Ballet Performance." *The Bermuda Sun Weekly* (June 20, 1970).

Reviews the Dance Theatre of Harlem.

1303. [W., J.S.] J.S.W. "Bubbles Revives Rarely Seen Sand Dance." *PM* (Mar. 19, 1942).

John W. Bubbles of the team Buck and Bubbles.

1304. [W., M.] M.W. "New Negro Art Theater in Debut as Dance." *New York Herald Tribune* (Apr. 30, 1931).

Edna Guy and Hemsley Winfield's group in its debut.

1305. Wahls, Robert. "Jo's Spaghetti Legs Whip up 'Jamaica' Gale." *New York Daily News* (Feb. 9, 1958).

Profiles Josephine Premice on the occasion of her appearance in the Broadway musical "Jamaica."

1306. Waldron, Clarence. "Stockton Takes in African Dance." *Sunday Press* [Atlantic City, N.J.] (Feb. 22, 1981).

Chuck Davis Dance Company at Stockton State College, Pomona, N.J.

1307. Walker, Danton. "Cabarabian Nights." *New York Daily News* (May 20, 1951).

Briefly discusses Pearl Primus and her accomplishments.

1308. Walrond, Eric. "Charleston, Hey! Hey!" *Vanity Fair* 26, no. 2 (1926): 73, 116.

The author attempts to trace the origin of the charleston and its trail to Harlem and the Midwest. Other dances mentioned are the scrontch and the black bottom.

1309. Walser, Richard. "His Worship the John Kuner." *North Carolina Folklore* 19, no. 4 (Nov. 1971): 160-72.

Discusses the John Canoe ritual in the West Indies and in N. C. Indicates it occurred widely in eastern N.C.

1310. Walsh, William S. *Curiosities of Popular Customs and of Rites, Ceremonies, Observances, and Miscellaneous Antiquities.* Philadelphia: J.B. Lippincott, 1897.

Gives an alphabetical listing of popular customs. Pinkster Day, celebrated at Whitsuntide in colonial times, became especially popular with blacks in Albany after the holiday was abandoned by whites. Its chief feature was the toto dance of African origin. It was danced to drum-like music and the steps included a double shuffle heel-toe breakdown.

1311. Walton, Lester A. "Harlem Negroes Introduce New Eclipse Dance." *New York Times* (Feb. 28, 1925).

1312.   Warner, Charles Dudley. *Studies in the South and West with Comments in Canada.* New York: Harper, 1889.

Describes New Orleans voodoo ceremonies and dancing in Chapter 4, "A Voudoo Dance" pp. 64-74.

1313.   Warren, Joyce. "Capitol Ballet Shows Confidence, Gaiety." *Evening Star* (June 1, 1968).

Reviews a performance of the Capitol Ballet Company at the Cramiton Auditorium, Howard University. Doris Jones and Claire Haywood are the founders.

1314.   ———. "Desires of a Black Ballerina: To Contribute; Not to Star." *Sunday Star* [Washington, D.C.] (Oct. 18, 1970).

Profiles Llanchie Stevenson of Dance Theatre of Harlem.

1315.   Warwick, Florence. "The Dance in the Negro College." *Dance Herald* (Dec. 1937).

Calls for the black college to give dance its rightful place in the curriculum as a fine art.

1316.   Washburn, Charles. "Bill Robinson Won Stockyards Boost in 'Balancing Act.'" *New York Herald Tribune* (Nov. 16, 1930).

Bill Robinson tells of his times pushing a truck in the Chicago stockyards.

1317.   Washington, Booker T. "Interesting People: Bert Williams." *American Magazine* 70 (1910): 600-04.

1318.   Washington, Fredi. "Jeni, the Piquant Go-Getter." *People's Voice* (Aug. 21, 1943): 24.

Profiles Jeni LeGon, singer-dancer on Broadway and in

Hollywood, upon her opening a dance school whose specialty was the precision dancing used in chorus lines.

1319. Watson, John F. *Annals of Philadelphia and Pennsylvania in the Olden Time: Being a Collection of Memoirs, Anecdote and Incidents of the City and Its Inhabitants....* Philadelphia: Elijah Thomas, 1857.

In vol. 2, pp. 261-66, the author comments on the Philadelphia "coloured" and includes a brief description of their dancing at fairs.

1320. Webster, Daniel. "Philadelphia Company Finds Its Feet: Arthur Hall's Afro-American Dance Ensemble Gains National Recognition." *Dance Magazine* 45 (July 1969): 62-64.

1321. Wenig, Adele R. *Pearl Primus: An Annotated Bibliography of Sources from 1943 to 1975.* Oakland, Calif.: Wenadance, Unlimited, 1983.

This bibliography lists books, periodicals, and visual materials. Periodicals and newspapers are arranged chronologically. Material is mainly from sources located in New York City, the base for Pearl Primus's activities.

1322. Wershba, Joseph. "The Gift of Healing Is Not Always a Medical Matter." *New York Post* (Aug. 9, 1960).

Profiles Pearl Primus.

1323. ———. "A Dancer Says Kindness is Killing the Negro Theater." *New York Post* (Mar. 28, 1962).

Geoffrey Holder gives his opinions on blacks and the arts.

1324. West, C.S.T. "The Human Condition: Dances with Rare Insight." *Daily World* (Mar. 16, 1983).

Reviews Eleo Pomare in a Dancemobile performance in New York City.

1325. "West Indian Wedding in New England." *Ebony* (Oct. 1955): 78-82.

Carmen De Lavallade and Geoffrey Holder wed in Conn.

1326. "What became of...Henry 'Crip' Heard." *Sepia* (Aug. 1960): 34.

Profile of a dancer missing a leg and an arm.

1327. Wharton, Linda and Jack L. Daniel. "Black Dance: Its African Origins and Continuity." *Minority Voices* 1 (no. 2): 73-80.

Explains the relationship of the traditional African world view and dance. States that "black dance is a vital cultural testament to the strength and survival of Africanisms that have been transplanted and uprooted but not transformed. The basic concepts of traditional African dance have survived among Africans the world over." Bibliography pp. 79-80.

1328. "Whatever Happened to...Peg Leg Bates." *Ebony* (Nov. 1973): 202).

1329. "What Happened to: Valda?" *Hue* (Dec. 1954): 46.

Tells what happened to the first black exotic dancer to work at Minsky's, the famous burlesque house.

1330. "What's Happening." *Ebony* (June 1978): 80-82.

Features Fred Berry, actor on the television show "What's Happening?" and a former Don Campbell Lock Dancer.

1331. "When She Dances, Rome Burns." *Our World* (Oct. 1954): 8-11.

Lavinia Hamilton, former Dunham dancer, becomes popular in a Rome night club performing authentic Caribbean, African, and blues dances.

1332. "Whites Come to Small's Paradise on Tuesdays to Do the Twist." *New York Amsterdam News* (Apr. 14, 1962): 1.

1333. Whitten, Norman E. Jr. and Aurelio Fuentes. "Baile Marimba! Negro Folk Music in Northwest Ecuador." *Journal of the Folklore Institute* 3, no. 2 (1966): 168-91.

The author describes and gives the social context of the major aspects of Ecuadoran marimba music and dance. Described are the musical instruments, dancers, dances, dancing, and the themes of marimba.

1334. Whitten, Norman E., Jr. "Música y Relaciones Sociales en las Tierras Bajas Colombianas y Ecudorianas del Pacífico: Estudio Sobre Micro-evolución Sociocultural." *América Indígena* 27 (1967): 635-65. Translated in English and reprinted as: "Personal Networks and Musical Contexts in the Pacific Lowlands of Colombia and Ecuador." *Man* 3 (1968): 50-63.

Discusses the marimba (currulao) and chigualo dances among the blacks of northwest Ecuador and southwest Colombia and how they reflect social relations.

1335. ———. *Black Frontiersmen: A South American Case.* New York: Schenkman Publishing Company, 1974.

An anthropological study of the Afro-Hispanic culture in the Pacific lowlands of Ecuador and Colombia. Dances relating to secular and sacred rituals are discussed in Chapters 5 and 6.

1336. ———. "Ritual Enactment of Sex Roles in the Pacific Lowlands of Ecuador-Colombia." *Ethnology* 13 (1974): 129-43.

Dance activities discussed are cantinas and baile marimbas (currulao).

1337. "Who to Tango?" *Central African Examiner* (June 18, 1960): 17.

Discusses the derivation of the Argentinean dance.

1338.   "Whose Twist Is It? Hank Ballard Says His." *New York Post*
             (Oct. 29, 1961).

             Ballard claims he composed the twist and was edged out by
             Chubby Checker.

1339.   Wiley, Maureen. "The Showcase Company." *Dance Dialogue*
             (Winter 1981): 12-13.

             Reviews a performance of Philadanco (Philadelphia Dance
             Company). Also decries the fact that Philadelphia does not support
             this company. As a result, its best dancers have left for other,
             financially established companies.

1340.   Wilkinson, Robert. "'Mass' Acclaimed for Emotional Impact."
             OSU Lantern [Ohio State University] (Apr. 20, 1974).

             Reviews Leonard Bernstein's "Mass," choreographed by Gus
             Solomons, Jr. at Ohio State University.

1341.   Williams, Charles H. *Cotton Needs Pickin': Characteristic Negro
             Folk Dances*. Norfolk, Va.: Guide Publishing Co., 1929.

             Illustrates eight black songs and dance steps with photographs.
             The eight dances are "Cotton Needs Pickin'," steps and rhythmic
             action characteristic of black life set to a work song; "Plantation
             Days," featuring the steps in the old country dance or "break
             down" common on plantations; charleston, with steps
             demonstrated by those remembering the dance from childhood;
             "Going Up the Mountain," "Granddaddy Is Dead," "Go In and Out
             the Window," and "Peep Squirrel," all singing games; and the May
             pole dance, the steps of which were used at a May Day festival at
             the Hampton Institute.

1342.   Williams, Joseph J. *Voodoos and Obeahs: Phases of West India
             Witchcraft*. New York: Dial Press, 1932.
             Studies in the origins of the development of voodoo in Haiti
             and obeah in Jamaica. Attempts to distinguish the truth about

voodoo and obeah. Describes dancing involved in the rituals of each.

1343. Williams, Julinda Lewis. "Black Dance: A Look at the State of the Art." *Black American* 20, no. 8 (1981).

Discusses the state of black dance and reviews the Dancemobile Winter Series, Feb. 1981. Companies reviewed were Dianne McIntyre's Sounds in Motion, International Afrikan-American Ballet, Philadanco, and Nanette Bearden Contemporary Dance Theatre.

1344. Williams, Peter. "The National Dance Theatre of Jamaica in London." *Dance and Dancers* (Nov. 1965): 23-37, 52.

Reviews the company's entire London season.

1345. ———. "On Their Way: Black New World." *Dance and Dancers* (Nov. 1967): 27-29.

Reviews a performance of Donald McKayle's "Black New World" at the Edinburgh Festival.

1346. Williams, Wilson. "Prelude to a Negro Ballet." *The American Dancer* (Mar. 1940): 14, 39.

Williams discusses the failure of black dancers and choreographers to fulfill their promise despite the great influence of black dance on the theater.

1347. Williamson, Liz and Mike Moore. "The Eclectic Elusive Dance Called Jazz." *Dance Magazine* 52, no. 2 (Feb. 1978): 63-75.

1348. Wilson, Arthur T. "Glenn Brooks Third World Movements Dance Company." *Black Creations* (Spring 1972): 48-49.

1349. ———. "Al Perryman: Dancer." *Black Creation* 4, no. 1 (Fall 1972): 38-41.

Interview and biographical sketch.

1350. ——. "Sparks." *Black Creation* (Winter 1972): 36.

Discusses the themes that black choreographers use. Should they only use "themes of blackness" or other more artistically important themes?

1351. ——. "Geechies: A Choreo-Poem for the Stage." *Attitude* (Apr. 1983): 7, 17.

Review of a Gregory Millard work produced by Dance Theatre Workshop.

1352. ——. "Jubilation! at Riverside." *Attitude* (Apr. 1983): 7.

Review of Kevin Jeff's Jubilation! Dance Company.

1353. ——. "Pepsi Bethel: Fire in His Soul and All that Jazz." *Attitude* (Sept./Oct. 1983): 3-6.

1354. ——. "Al Perryman: The Stardust Road of a Veteran Hoofer." *Attitude* 2, no. 6 (Nov. 1983): 19-20.

1355. Wilson, John S. "Avon Long a Hit in 'Porgy and Bess' Role He Refused to Understudy 6 Years Ago." *PM* (Mar. 4, 1942).

Profiles Long on the occasion of his performance of Sportin' Life in "Porgy and Bess."

1356. ——. "A Vibrant Josephine Premice Returns." *New York Times* (Apr. 26, 1966).

Reviews her act at the East 74th Street Theater.

1357. Wilson, John A. "Unusual Combination of Dances Closes Philadelphia Folk Fete." *New York Times* (Sept. 1, 1970).

Reviews the Afro-American Dance Ensemble at the Philadelphia Folk Festival.

1358. Wilson, Robert. "Audience Eats up 'Fat Tuesday.'" *Memphis Press-Scimitar* (Feb. 18, 1977).

Arthur Hall Afro-American Dance Ensemble performance of "Fat Tuesday (and All that Jazz)" produced by the Tennessee Performing Arts Foundation.

1359. Wimble, Barton. "Harlem Ballet Has One Hit, One Strike." *New York News* (Jan. 11, 1980).

A review of the Dance Theatre of Harlem's American première of Glen Tetley's "Greening" and "Swan Lake" Act II.

1360. ———. "Philadelphia in Brooklyn." *New York News* (Dec. 8,.1980).

Reviews Philadanco performing at Brooklyn College.

1361. ———. "Mainly Masterly." *New York News* (Jan. 15, 1981).

Review of the Dance Theatre of Harlem performing "Greening," "Swan Lake" Act II, "The Greatest," and "Troy Game."

1362. Winer, Linda. "Holder's 'Banda' Ballet is a Voodoo Dazzler." *New York News* (Jan. 21, 1982).

Dance Theatre of Harlem premières Geoffrey Holder's work.

1363. ———. "Harlem Company's 'Frankie and Johnny.'" *New York News* (Jan. 28, 1982).

Dance Theatre of Harlem.

1364. ———. "A Celebration of Feet." *New York News* (Feb. 14, 1982).

Discusses the current revival of tap dancing after it was almost lost as an art. Also mentions the performers in "Tappin' Uptown" at the Brooklyn Academy of Music.

1365. Wingfield, Roland. "New Orleans Marching Bands: A Choreographer's Delight." *Dance Magazine* 33 (Jan. 1959): 34-35.

Describes street dancers following a New Orleans marching band.

1366. Winslow, Thyra Samter. "The Charleston—30 Years After." *Dance Magazine* (Jan. 1955): 26-33.

Discusses possible origins of the charleston and black bottom.

1367. Winter, Marian Hannah. "Juba and American Minstrelsy." In *Chronicles of the American Dance* edited by Paul D. Magriel, 38-63. New York: Henry Holt, 1948. Also in *Dance Index* no. 6 (1947): 28-49.

Uses the life of William Henry Lane (Juba) as a focal point in showing the importance of minstrel dances and their sources to jazz and tap dance.

1368. Wolowic, Jill. "Artist Re-Teaches Primal Movement." *OSU* [Ohio State University] *Lantern* (Apr. 19, 1974).

Profiles Gus Solomons, Jr., artist-in-residence at Ohio State University.

1369. Woltman, Frederick. "King of the Savoy." *Negro Digest* (July 1951): 95-97. Reprinted from the *New York World-Telegram*, Feb. 10, 1951.

A sketch of Charles Buchanan, manager of the Savoy Ballroom.

1370. "Women in the News." *New York Amsterdam News* (Dec. 16, 1950): 22.

Announces that Janet Collins received the 1950 Merit Award from *Mademoiselle* as having made a distinctive mark in her field.

1371. Woody, Regina Llewellyn (Jones). *Student Dancer.* Boston: Houghton Mifflin, 1951.

This novel, written for teenagers, describes the summer that the main character spends in New York studying dance. Describes her visits to the Katherine Dunham school.

1372. Woolf, S.J. "Bill Robinson, 60, Taps out the Joy of Living." *New York Times Magazine* (May 22, 1938).

1373. "World's First All-Negro Ballet." *Downbeat Chicago* (Dec. 1937): 48.

News brief with photo reports on the debut of the American Negro Ballet at New York's LaFayette Theater.

1374. Wright, Arthur. *Color Me White.* Smithtown, N.Y.: Exposition Press, 1980.

Autobiography of a dancer who danced with Katherine Dunham, Martha Graham, and Jean-Léon Destiné, among others. Focuses on Smith's career and on his disease, vitiligo.

1375. Wright, Patricia. "The Prime of Miss Pearl Primus." *Contact* [University of Massachusetts at Amherst] 10, no. 3 (Feb. 1985): 13-16.

Discusses Primus's career and her love of African dance.

1376. Wright, Richardson. *Revels in Jamaica, 1682-1838.* New York: Dodd, Mead, 1937.

A history of Jamaican social life that describes John Canoe festivities (pp. 239-41) and set-girls (pp. 243-47). Throughout are passing references to dancing.

1377. Writers Project, Georgia. *Drums and Shadows.* Athens, Ga.: University of Georgia Press, 1940.

Georgia coastal blacks are interviewed about folk customs and beliefs. Many speak of dances and the occasions on which they are performed. Some of the dances mentioned: buzzard lope, camel walk, Come Down to the Mire, fish bone, fish tail, and snake hips.

1378.   Writers Program. New York. *Negroes of New York: The Dance.* [New York, 1936-40].

Research studies compiled by workers of the Writers Program of the Works Projects Administration.

1379.   Wynter, Sylvia. "Jonkonnu in Jamaica: Toward the Interpretation of Folk Dances as Cultural Process." *Jamaica Journal* 4, no. 2 (June 1970): 34-48.

Discusses the origin and describes the John Canoe and myalism ceremonies in Jamaica. Suggests that although John Canoe was tolerated as harmless fun and myalism was driven underground as dangerous, they both contain the same elements.

1380.   Yarborough, Lavinia Williams. *Haiti-Dance.* Frankfurt-am-Main: Brönners Druckerie, n.d.

Gives a brief account of Lavinia Williams's involvement as a teacher and founder of the Haitian Institute of Folklore and Classic Dance.

1381.   ———. "Haiti, where I Teach Dance." *Dance Magazine* (Oct. 1956): 42-44, 76-79.

1382.   ———. *Ballet d'Haiti.* Port-au-Prince: Panorama, 1973.

Introduction briefly describes the career of Lavinia Williams. Gives a glossary of terms used in voodoo rites and dance and describes the repertoire of Ballets d'Haiti, which includes the dances of the rada, congo, and petro rites and various carnivals and secular dances.

1383.   Yarbrough, Camille. "Black Dance in America: The Old Seed." *Black Collegian* (Nov. 1980): 46-48, 50, 53.

1384. ———. "Black Dance in America: The Deep Root and the Strong Branch." *Black Collegian* (Apr.-May 1981): 10, 12, 14-24.

1385. Yearwood, Linda. "The Mamas, Papas and Kids Shake a Happy Hip." *New York Amsterdam News* (Jan. 29, 1983): 23.

   The La Rocque Bey School of Dance Theater in New York City.

1386. "Young American Dancers 'Take Over' Hunter Stage." *Daily Compass* (Jan. 18, 1952).

   Donald McKayle at the Hunter Playhouse.

1387. Ziegler, Jan. "Some Blacks Claim Discrimination in Ballet." *Tennessean* (July 16, 1981).

1388. Zimmer, Diane. "Katherine Dunham, a Biography." *Dance Book Forum* 1 (1981): 20-21.

   A review of Ruth Beckford's biography of Dunham with reflections by Charles Moore and Pearl Reynolds on their relationship with Dunham.

1389. Zolotow, Maurice. "South of the Border on Broadway." *New York Times Magazine* (Feb. 18, 1940).

   Discusses the popularity of dances like the conga, rumba, and samba.

ADDENDA

1390. Ahye, Molly. *Cradle of Caribbean Dance: Beryl McBurnie and the Little Carib Theatre.* Petit Valley, Trinidad and Tobago: Heritage Cultures, Ltd., 1983.

Historical account of the contribution of Beryl McBurnie to Caribbean dance.

1391. "Negro Ballet's Immediate Impact." *The Northern Echo* [Newcastle, England] (Sept. 17, 1957).

Reviews a performance of the New York Negro Ballet in Newcastle.

1392. "Negro Dances in Arkansas." *Journal of American Folk Lore* 1 (1888): 83.

This reprint from the *Boston Herald* of May 7, 1887, describes dances done around a grave by a congregation trying to raise their dead pastor.

Arthur Hall Afro-American Dance Ensemble *see* Afro-American Dance Ensemble
Association of Black Choreographers 200, 939
Aul, Ronne 594, 1129
Austin, Debra 238
Authentic Jazz Theater (*see also* Bethel, Pepsi) 138
Awasa (Dutch Guiana) 610, 1065

Bahamas 636, 638, 1061
Bailey, Bill 102, 181, 368, 676, 991, 1241, 1242
Baion 262
Baker, Josephine 643, 680, 787, 915, 1072, 1078, 1180
Baker, Shawneequa *see* Scott, Shawneequa Baker
Ballet 22, 111, 112, 126, 150, 212, 456, 617, 632, 648, 801, 820, 822, 914, 920, 937, 959, 967, 969, 970, 983, 1138, 1182, 1203, 1208, 1252, 1346, 1391
History of 26 Companies 1, 101, 133, 198, 477, 482, 484, 993, 1312, 1373
Ballet Americana *see* New York Negro Ballet
Ballet Folklorico Dominicano 675
Ballet d'Haiti 380
Ballet Negres 173
Ballroom Dancing 407, 475, 953
Balls 237, 385, 495, 948, 949, 950 Quadroon Balls 86, 88, 624, 749, 946
Baltimore Dance Theatre 53
Bamboula 263, 416, 823, 1274

Bambuco 1066
Bambula 288, 1042, 1043
Banda 639
Bandamba 610, 692, 1065
Banks, Marilyn 33, 444
Barbados 14, 385, 401
Barton, James 1216
Barry, Ken 629
Bassa Moona 157
Bates, Clayton (Peg Leg) 928, 1037, 1038, 1110, 1328
Battle, Hinton 447
Batucada 94
Batuque 288, 782, 1043
Baylay *see* Bélé
Beatty, Talley 125, 148, 423, 451, 540, 593, 605, 645, 861, 897, 1279
Be Bop 159
Beguine *see* Biguine
Belaire *see* Bélé
Bélé 9, 19, 172, 375, 392, 581, 612, 777, 888, 889
Belize 799
Belle Rosette *see* McBurnie, Beryl
Benjamin, Fred (*see also* Fred Benjamin Dance Company) 793
Bennett, Joe 12
Bermuda 385, 391
Bernice Johnson Dance Company 21
Berry Brothers 571, 1272
Berry, Fred 845, 1330
Berry, James 389, 390
Bethel, Pepsi (*see also* Authentic Jazz Theater) 138, 1353
Bey, La Rocque *see* La Rocque Bey's Dancers and Drummers

489, 545, 934, 1055, 1059,
1109, 1201, 1213, 1278
Calenda *see* Calinda
Calinda 9, 42, 71, 172, 209, 263,
288, 338, 468, 469, 581, 754,
948, 949, 950, 972, 1042, 1043,
1189, 1274, 1312
Calypso 262, 327, 351, 421,
460, 488, 1001,
Camel Walk 1377
Campbell, Don 818
Campbell Lock Dancers 818,
845
Candombe 77, 228, 273, 288,
290, 823, 1042, 1043, 1121
Candomble 269, 881
Cane-Cutting 495
Canned Apple 1159
Cantina 1336
Capitol Ballet 154, 1143, 1313
Capoeira 41, 280, 291, 323, 499,
756, 766, 941, 979, 1089, 1133
Carabiné 495
Caribbean 94, 172, 177, 427,
432, 537, 546, 671, 715, 781,
913, 1163, 1186, 1195, 1390
Caribbean Cultural Center 382
Caribs, Black 331, 688, 1195
Carioca 262
"Carmina Burana" 598
Carnival 146, 337, 350, 581,
1087 Brazil 408, 512, 1273 Rio
De Janeiro 289, 532 Haiti 1176
Trinidad 9, 19, 351, 385, 471
Uruguay 287, 289
Carriacou 283, 1088, 1190
Castillian 9
Castle, Vernon and Irene 71,
470

Catherine Market (New York
City) 397
Central America 81
Cha-Cha 262, 300, 953, 1000,
1023
Chapman, Gary 203
Charleston 71, 221, 262, 381,
387, 410, 530, 656, 750, 779,
952, 1155, 1308, 1341, 1366
Chauvet, Norma 968
Checker, Chubby 311, 472,
1153
Chiaviano, Olga 829
Chica 288, 1042, 1043
Chicken 305
Chicken Scratch 978, 1050
Chiffone 9
Chilton and Thomas 306
Chilton, Carol 306
Chirrup 9
Choreographers 6, 38, 121,
136, 200, 201, 266, 308, 356,
411, 413, 448, 461, 559, 721,
747, 846, 896, 939, 1007, 1123,
1164, 1165, 1174, 1350
Directory 201
Choreo-Mutation 25
Chorus Lines 309, 336, 454,
541, 1071, 1263, 1318
Christmas 165, 233, 385, 391,
405, 495, 537, 788, 844, 1018,
1085, 1195, 1223, 1297
Chryst, Gary 885
Chuck Davis Dance Company
312, 578, 1181 Reviews 54,
179, 272, 275, 708, 867, 899,
905, 1306
Cimber, Alphonse 64, 810
Cincinatti Ballet 734

Dance Teams 306, 407, 711,
1216, 1264 Comedy 1214
Dance Theatre of Harlem 4,
15, 126, 141, 206, 324, 383,
445, 446, 452, 446, 522, 544,
566, 567, 659, 742, 745, 882,
886, 932, 1026, 1039, 1075,
1119, 1131, 1166, 1314
Reviews 16, 17, 22, 61, 63, 67,
133, 134, 139, 140, 143, 144,
158, 486, 487, 533, 534, 535,
536, 565, 605, 609, 666, 684,
702, 738, 741, 744, 767, 924,
985, 1101, 1120, 1302, 1359,
1361, 1362, 1363
Dance Therapy 1261
DanceAfrica 264
Dancemobile 34, 35, 37, 39, 68,
69, 359, 902, 1168, 1324, 1343
Dancing (General) 5, 25, 31, 81,
103, 211, 231, 245, 259, 261,
316, 320, 324, 378, 425, 428,
497, 562, 821, 863, 923, 964,
1093, 1111, 1183, 1196, 1260,
1315, 1345, 1346 Bibliography
18, 649 Discrimination 124, 677,
712, 963, 1111 History 207,
221, 243, 261, 463, 465, 526,
570, 657, 703, 763, 823, 943,
1047, 1198, 1201, 1280, 1277,
1383, 1384, 1387 Pictorial
Works 339, 1057, 1237
Daniel 672
Danz, Inc. 69
"Darktown Follies" 1215
Dave, Peggy 1064
Davila, Angela 527
Davis, Altovise 203

Davis, Chuck (*see also* Chuck
Davis Dance Company) 1181,
1224
Davis, George 623
Davis, Hazel Thompson 247
Davis, Ron (*see also* Ron Davis
Dancers) 119, 681
Davis, Toots 1215
Day, Diane 203
Dayton Contemporary Dance
Company 753
D.C. Black Repertory Dance
Company 491
Dean, Dora 267, 414, 545, 1288
Dehn, Mura 1006
de Joie, Norman 1021
De Lavallade, Carmen 95, 109,
162, 276, 277, 362, 375, 603,
738, 893, 894, 927, 960, 962,
981, 982, 1136, 1279, 1290,
1325
De Lavallade, Yvonne 78
DeLoatch, Gary 33
De Paur, Starletta 295
Destine, Bob 213
Destiné, Jean-Léon 50, 370,
395, 396, 556, 597, 723, 810,
1049, 1161, 1257, 1374
Detroit City Dance Company
40, 792
Dickerson, Liz 307
Dinizulu, Gus 99, 1183
Disco Dancing 483, 507, 615,
1114, 1144
Discrimination *see* Dancing
(General), Discrimination
Dominican Republic 335, 382,
400, 488, 782, 783, 807
Dominican Street Dancers 382
Dominicana, La 455

Twist 302, 311, 472, 517, 563, 620, 1023, 1238, 1287, 1332, 1338

United States 94, 1051, 1111, 1367
Uruguay 273, 288, 287, 290, 786, 1041, 1042, 1043

Valda 1329
Van Heerden, Augustus 227, 478, 712
Vaudeville 489, 667, 839, 1063, 1278
Velorio de la Cruz 9
Venezuela 180, 282, 780, 782, 802, 803
Vereen, Ben 166, 197, 203, 252, 318, 419, 701, 748, 790, 878, 880, 995, 1022, 1073, 1084, 1105, 1107, 1269
Verna, Anita 813
Virgin Islands 416, 777, 780, 783, 989
Virginia 330, 492, 1204
Virginia Essence 838, 1283
Virginia Reel 584
Visionary Dance 229
Vodu *see* Voodoo
Vodun *see* Voodoo
Von Grona, Eugene 66, 270, 481, 791, 835, 850, 1115, 1116, 1167
Voodoo 269, 357, 394, 569, 911, 1231, 1256, 1300, 1312, 1362
Haiti 50, 229, 337, 355, 394, 433, 435, 498, 611, 638, 639, 916, 918, 922, 1148, 1177, 1178, 1257, 1342, 1382 New

Orleans 71, 86, 88, 294, 583, 1239, 1312

WPA 151, 195
Walker, Aida Overton 250
Walker, George 250, 574
Wanáragua 331, 709, 1195
Washington, Norma 115
Webb, Margot *see* Norton and Margot
Wells, Dickie 399
Welsh, Carole Kariamu 27
West Indies 14, 172, 278, 385, 432, 471, 537, 546, 569, 581, 760, 777, 890, 975, 989, 1013, 1195, 1235, 1309
White, Myrna 944
Whitman, Alice 926
Whitman Sisters 926
Wilkinson, Raven 150, 937, 1016, 1138, 1292, 1301
Williams and Walker (*see also* Walker, George; Williams, Bert) 574, 1213, 1278
Williams, Bert 250, 632, 1084, 1317
Williams, Charles H. 847
Williams, Dudley 440, 608
Williams, Ethel 1215
Williams, Lavinia 89, 163, 224, 258, 355, 380, 423, 671, 715, 716, 764, 774, 775, 776, 805, 841, 968, 1012, 1062, 1095, 1162, 1209, 1380, 1382
Williams, Ruth 1211, 1247
Williams, Wilson 762, 879, 1346
Wilson, Billy 38, 356, 461
Wilson, Lester 1007